Walter Stanhope

Monastic London

Walter Stanhope

Monastic London

ISBN/EAN: 9783337397340

Printed in Europe, USA, Canada, Australia, Japan

Cover: Foto ©Lupo / pixelio.de

More available books at **www.hansebooks.com**

MONASTIC LONDON

AN ANALYTICAL SKETCH

OF THE

Monks and Monasteries within the
Metropolitan Area during the
Centuries 1200 to 1600

BY

WALTER STANHOPE

London

REMINGTON & CO., PUBLISHERS

HENRIETTA STREET, COVENT GARDEN

1887

CONTENTS

——:o:——

	PAGE
PREFACE	7

PART FIRST

| GENERAL SURVEY . . . . | 15 |

PART SECOND

| COMMENTARY ON THE MONKS OF OLD | 43 |

PART THIRD

| DIGEST OF THE LONDON RELIGIOUS HOUSES . | 105 |

| INDEX . . . . . | 163 |

PREFACE

—:o:—

It has been well said, that a writer of the present day must be continually at fault in attempting to reproduce, upon a modern stage, ancient times, ancient humankind and ancient customs. To pry into the depths of an almost fathomless antiquity, or to make any attempt to drain the fountain of antiquarian research is a task beyond human skill and human labour.

In the era whereof we write, a vast change was on the eve of taking place in England. The well-beaten paths trodden by the footsteps of centuries were being uprooted. Old things were passing away—the faith and life of ages gone were dissolving like the unsubstantial pageantry of a dream. Chivalry was beginning to expire—to our irremediable social loss in this age, it seems to have altogether become extinct—while the feudal castle as well as the peaceful monastery was doomed to destruction. All the manners, customs, beliefs, convictions, and desires of the past were fleeing before the advent of those heralding the future.

The change, then in its primary throes, has long since been fully consummated, and between England of the present day, and that of the middle ages, there lies a gulf of mystery and profundity which the prose of the historian or the fancy of the romance writer, will never satisfactorily rebridge. Those feudal days and those feudal organizations cannot unite with us, nor can our imagination, with any precision, penetrate back to them.

Although it does not become the writers of a great nation to indulge in bluster or rhodomantade, yet there can be no urgent reason why they should smother their convictions and stifle every sense of right and justice. Moreover, it is neither fair nor just to blame lightly sentiments and conduct that were the offspring of events, which are, and indeed only can be, imperfectly understood in modern times.

We are, let us be thankful, out-living the gross prejudices, which in a bygone age repre-

sented Monastic life as being from first to last
an existence of laziness, dissoluteness and
imposture. We now-a-days acknowledge that,
but for the monks of old, 'the glorious lights
of Liberty, Literature and Science,' which awoke
the world anew, as of old, Sol did Chaos, might
have remained for ever dead and unnurtured.
We must testify this much further, that, but
for them and their magnificent cloistral homes
during more than six centuries, there would
have existed no safe haven for the devout, the
gentle, the thoughtful, and the oppressed
throughout the land.

We have, therefore, endeavoured to write
without bias of these monks of old, believing
that in any narrative, however concise, the
suppressio veri would be only a step removed
from the *suggestio falsi*, so that while demon-

strating that the monkish calling was upheld by its doctrinals as 'a medicine for life and immortality,' we have sought to test that principle by detailing something of its internal economy and of its obsolete manners and customs. We have in a measure garnished our dry recitals by adding thereto—

'Old legends of the monkish page,
Traditions of the saint and sage,
Tales that have the rime of age
And chronicles of old.'

It is, however, no loving, lingering picture— which to the devout ascetic of antiquity proved so oft the perfection of earthly bliss—we have attempted. We have only striven to render a vivid account of cloistral existence, when Monachism, after being anchored for more than one thousand years in the great stream of

Time, was at last in danger of shipwreck and utter ruin.

The monstrous crimes of earlier ages may, it has been asserted, find mercy in consideration of the pollution and darkness of the moral atmosphere in which men lived and sinned. If that argument be considered of weight to excuse the unmatched sins of the laity, it must tell with more formidable force in favour of those cenobites, who were the pioneers of all that is noble, grand and glorious in Science Literature or Art.

This modest contribution may be the more acceptable since the republication of the Count de Montalembert's great and most interesting work. That republication must create additional interest in the subject of Monachism, and consequently a less ambitious effort in the shape of an analysis or digest may find favour and acceptance with the studious. Such, at all events, is the Author's hope, as it is his apology for submitting this work to public reference and inquisition.

Part First

General Survey

Monastic London

GENERAL SURVEY

In the following commentary the author has given some descriptive details of the monks of old, and in the succeeding digest a short analytical compendium of their homes within the Metropolitan area. In this first part of his work he proposes to render to his readers some precise information respecting the system as a whole.

In referring, however cursorily, to the different orders of monks, precedence must be

B

given to the founders, after whom mention will
be made of the martyrs, then of the royal saints,
and lastly of the canonized saints of both sexes,
giving rank according to their celebrity and
popularity. From the following list then have
sprung all the acknowledged orders of cloistral
devotees who have ever yoked themselves
together in religious brotherhood.

First.—St Benedict, who is the general
patriarch of all the Benedictine communities,
and under whom rank St Romnaldo, founder
of the Camaldolesi; St John Gualberto, founder
of the Vallambrosians; St Parmo, founder of
the Carthusians; and St Bernard, founder of
the Cistercians.

Second.—St Augustine of Hippo, the general
patriarch of all Augustine Communities, and
under whom rank, St Philip Benozzi, founder of
the Servi; St Peter Nolasco, founder of the
Order of Mercy; St Bridget of Sweden, founder
of the Brigittines; and St Joseph, a patriarch
and general patron of the Augustines.

Third.—St Francis, the general patriarch of
the Franciscans, Capuchins, Observants, Conventuals, Minimes, and other orders, and under

whom rank St Dominick, founder of the
Dominicans or preaching friars; St Albert of
Vercelli, founder of the Carmelites; St Jerome,
founder of the Jeronymites; and St Ignatius
Loyola, founder of the Jesuits.

Of these last, the Franciscans, the Dominicans, and the Carmelites, were the three great
mendicant orders, and sprang into existence
nearly simultaneously in the beginning of the
thirteenth century. The Franciscans and
Dominicans were from the first to have a
different destination from every other order.*
They were, as it may be termed, the spiritual
democrats; they were to mingle with the people,
yet without being of the people; they were to
take cognizance of all private and public affairs,
of all those domestic concerns and sympathies,
duties and pleasures from which their vows cut
them off. They were to possess nothing they
could call their own, either as a body, or
individually. They were to beg from their
fellow Christians food and raiment—such at
least was their original rule, a rule soon
modified, as we shall show. Their creative

* Curzon's Monasteries of the Levant.

vocation was to look after the stray sheep of
the fold of Christ; to pray with those who
prayed, to weep with those who wept, to preach
glad tidings, to exhort to repentance, to rebuke
sin and Satan, to advise the doubtful and
comfort the weak without distinction of place
or person. The privilege of ministering in the
offices of the Church was not theirs at first, but
was after a time conceded. They at first
practised all the stratagems of itineracy, preaching in the public streets, and administering the
Eucharist or Communion on a portable altar.
They were not to be called *Padri*, fathers, but
fratri, brothers, of all men; and when the
Dominicans assumed the title of *Fratri Pre-
dicatori*—preaching brothers—Francis in his
humility, is said to have at once styled his
community *Fratri minori, Frères mineurs*—
Minorites or lesser brothers. In England, from
the colour of their habits, these twin orders in
course of time, came to be designated the Black
Friars and the Grey Friars, names which they
have bequeathed to certain familiar districts in
London.

The mendicant orders were by far the

most popular, and of these the Dominicans
were as a body the most learned and ener-
getic. Their greatest canonized saints were
men who had raised themselves to eminence
by learning, by eloquence, by vigorous intel-
lect and resolute action. Of such, were St
Dominick, the founder, St Peter, martyr, St
Thomas Aquinas, the angelic doctor of laws,
St Raymond, St Antonio the good archbishop
of Florence, St Catharine of Sienna, St Peter
Gonzalez, St Pius—Pope Pius the Fifth, and St
Vincent of Ferraris. St Dominick was born
at Calagara, in the diocese of Osma, in the
kingdom of Castile, in the year 1160.* Both
his father and mother were of noble birth. He
originated the Rosary, and instituted the 'Third
Order of Penitence.' He died at Bologna in
1221, and was canonized by Gregory the Ninth,
in 1223. Friar Bacon, the *Doctor Mirabilis* or
Wonderful Doctor, who first lighted the torch
of science, near upon 600 years ago, was a
Franciscan. The Dominicans, out of their body,
produced two of the greatest painters of their
day, and indeed of many ages, Angelico da

* Legends of the Monastic Orders.

Fiesole and Bartolomeo della Porta, whose paintings remain to the present age the delight and wonder of the civilised world. Of this order Sir James Stephen writes—'In an age of oligarchal tyranny, they were the protectors of the weak, in an age of ignorance, the instructors of mankind, and in an age of profligacy, the stern vindicators of the holiness of the sacerdotal character and the sanctity of domestic life.

Though professing poverty—'the dame to whom none openeth pleasure's gate more than to death'—and originally ordained to toil, they felt few of its evils, for everyone gave of their substance to them. Faustus, the countryman, is made to say :—

'We give wool and chese, our wives coyne and eggs
When *freres* flatter and praise their proper legges.'

And a little further on he adds :—

' Phillis gave coyne because he did her charm,
Ever sith that time less hath she felt of harme.'

Speed remarks that every householder paid to each of the five orders of friars one penny per quarter, the amount of which contribution, being £43,333, 6s 8d per annum was equal to a fourth of the gross revenues of all the other religious orders as set forth by that author. But still they for the most part affected poverty if they did not suffer it. They sought to imitate the rare examples of Elisha and Elias, whom they asserted were friars and poor preachers such as they.

The habit of the Dominicans was a white woollen gown, fastened round the waist with a white girdle, over which lay a white scapular— a piece of cloth hanging down from the neck to the feet, like a long apron before and behind— while over all was worn a black cloak with long sleeves and a hood. The white in this habit was intended to denote purity of life, the black, mortification and penance. It was alleged to have been selected by the Blessed Virgin herself in a vision to one of the brethren, a monk of Orleans.*

In the early part of the century succeeding their institution the Dominicans and Franciscans perceiving they would be more respected

* Legends of the Monastic Orders.

and possess greater power, if they owned less
poverty and exhibited less humility, renounced
their more lowly estate and appearance, inducted sweeping innovations into their dwelling-
places and style of living, and in most respects
closely assimilated themselves to the other
great orders in the temples of pride and wealth.

The sanctuaries to which these remodelled
holy mendicants retreated were each a miniature
Goshen, enjoying the calm light of peace and
immunity, amid a scene of general confusion,
blood, and unremitted outrage in the world
beyond their cloistral walls. They thereafter
became so popular that many exceptional in-
dulgencies were granted by the Church of
Rome. For instance, they were exempted from
all Episcopal authority, were permitted to
preach or hear confessions without leave of the
ordinary, to accept legacies and to inter in their
churches. Pope Boniface the Eighth, in the
year 1295, fully and peremptorily established
these privileges. As a sequence, both Dominicans and Franciscans vied with each other in
lauding and magnifying the papal power and
supremacy.

It may be here generally asserted that monastic institutions and monastic buildings, like the Roman temples, were erected and endowed by the gifts of the rich and noble and, though more seldom, by the alms of the people, as well as by a subtraction of a portion of the revenues originally intended to have been devoted to very different purposes.

How sumptuous and noble some of their churches were, we have unimpeachable testimony in many of our cathedral and ecclesiastical structures of the present day—notably in Westminster Abbey, which was erected by monks and was the centre of the largest monachal institution in the metropolis.

The ensemble of the configuration of their interiors were magnificent in the extreme. The massy cylindrical columns and strong semicircular arches dividing the great nave from the uniformly welded aisles, together with the comparative rudeness perhaps of the transepts, combined with the oratories, Lady chapels, chantries, Galilee chapels, crypts, chancels and lofty triforium must have struck the beholder with many commingled feelings of awe and

wonder, devotion and admiration. They were
in those august times grand in their associations
with the most popular and fondly cherished
delusions, awful too with the most imposing and
stirring legends of mediæval mythology. A
forest glade of exquisitely wrought pillars reach-
ing from end to end on either side of the vast
and lofty naves, resembling from the extreme
western end, in very truth a scene of animated
nature itself—a plain, a forest and a sky of
stone—terminated by the high altar wondrously
enriched as the glorious tabernacles of their
titular saints, glowing in sombre magnificence
like a sunset at the extreme line of the mighty
perspective. The doorways lavishly sculptured
in shaft, capital and arch. The windows orna-
mented with chevron and zig-zag. The lofty
ceiling painted, gilded and panelled—the inter-
sections glowing with the armorial bearings of
the rich donors, by whose liberality and patronage the rare work had been carried to such
perfection, while the walls were doubtless
covered with the rarest examples of the limner's
art that the ancient and splendid epicureanism
of the Romish religion could conjure up.

We have little doubt from all we are able to glean that the interiors of the most celebrated churches were dazzling and imposing in the extreme, and that their chaste splendour must have instinctively inspired wonder and admiration in all who beheld their glories for the first time,—

> 'The granite columns, mountain high,
> Rose up defiant to the sky.'

while—

> 'The light,
> Through the rich gloom of pictur'd windows flowing,
> Tinged with soft awfulness a lovely sight.'

Another poet's rhyming will seem equally appropriate,—

> 'Here you stand,
> Adore and worship when you know it not,
> Pious above the meaning of your thought—
> Devout beyond the intention of your will.'

The Dominicans or preaching friars always had a splendid reputation as artists and *littérateurs* and as patrons of both. As an instance of the former we may mention that Nicolo Pisano was their greatest architect, while as evidence of the latter it may be stated they employed the following famed artists to decorate their churches — Titian, Leonardo da Vinci, Angelico, Fra Bartolomeo, Cigoli, Santi di Tito, Andrea Orcagna, Michael Angelo, Angelico da Fiesole, and Simon Memmi, whose individual works still stand distributed amid the shrines to which they were conveyed, as lasting evidences of their taste.

Recurring to our imaginary description of these palaces of art, let us proceed up the naves and in spirit enter the choir, beneath a low-curtained doorway under the organ-loft and awaiting our inspection is ecclesiastical magnificence in its richest and rarest form—a very Pactolus of wealth and beauty. We then approach the high altar whose blazonry consists of gold and silver, of alabaster and lapis-lazuli, of rare and precious marbles. There are the wide steps before that sumptuous altar whereon in those days knelt gentle and simple, while offering up prayers and vows that possessed at least the merit of being sincere. There stood the rarely enmarbled shrine, surmounted by its five crosses of carved work set with jewels, on the centre one thereof,—

' A bleeding Christ was raised
Of iv'ry wrought from types of diamonds bright,
Inlaid in gold a sparkling " I.N.R.I.," blazed
From every gem a drop of twinkling light,
Shot hues of rainbows on the dazzled sight,
Like glitter on the reliquary play'd,
Imbost with sculptures of that heav'nly fight,
When fell a show'r of Hosts in arms array'd,
Through Chaos and his realm of anarchy dismay'd.'*

Every monastery, as every village church in
ancient times had its special relics, its special
images, its especial attribute to attract public
interest and patronage—for the most part
the rare offerings of their numerous votaries.
On this subject we quote a passage from
a modern historian—' The reverence for the
remains of noble and pious men, the dresses
which they had worn on the bodies in which
their spirits had lived was in itself a natural and
pious emotion. It had been petrified into a
dogma, and like every other imaginative feeling
which is submitted to that process, it had
become a falsehood, a mere superstition, a
substitute for piety, not a stimulus to it and a
perpetual occasion for fraud. The people

* Fosbrooke's British Monachism, 394.

brought offerings to the shrines where it was
supposed that the relics were of greatest potency.
The clergy to secure the offerings invented relics
and invented the stories of the wonders which
had been worked by them. The great exposure
of these things took place at the visitation of
the religious houses * * * * Besides matters
of this kind there were images of the Virgin or
of the Saints, above all, roods or crucifixes of
special potency, the virtues of which had begun
to grow uncertain, however, to sceptical Protestants, and from doubt to denial and from
denial to passionate hatred, there were but a few
brief steps. The most famous of the roods was
that of Boxley, in Kent, which used to smile
and bow or frown and shake its head as its
worshippers were generous or close handed.
There was another, however, at Dovercourt, in
Suffolk of scarcely inferior fame. This image
was of such power, it was said that the door of
the church in which it stood was open at all
hours to all comers, and no human hand could
close it. Dovercourt, therefore, became a place
of great and lucrative pilgrimage much resorted
to by the neighbours on all occasions of

difficulty.'* Among these sacred repositories, we are assured, were such things simulated as the parings of St Edmund's toes, some ashes that had roasted St Lawrence, the girdle of the Blessed Virgin shown in several places, two or three heads of St Ursula, part of the under raiment of Thomas à Beckett, much reverenced by women, and earth from Golgotha and Calvary.

We cannot take exception to the dogma that there is an irresistible tendency in the course of human affairs to mix the tragic with the comic, the grave with the gay, and the sublimest questions with the most ridiculous mimicries. It was so evidently in the times and under the order of things whereto we refer. They may not have thought it, but most certainly the priests of those days acted as if they endeavoured to make religion a species of drama, farce or ballet, upon the supposition and with the intent most probably, that it would more vividly impress the imagination. They no doubt bethought themselves that there were sights which the human mind could not forget,

Froude's History of England, vol. ii, p. 91.

when once it had witnessed them, however much
it might thereafter desire to do so. An odd
figure, an imposing piece of mechanism, a
grotesque dress, an eccentric manner, a motley
procession, in fact, any outrage against good taste
or sound judgment, they assumed, easily took
possession of the mind and would not away
speedily with the things that are forgotten.
Pomp and ostentation of the most sacrilegious
kind and imposition of the rankest sort were
not held in disesteem by these priests or monks
of old.

> ' Christ everywhere thrust clear aside
> By mammon, priestcraft, pomp and pride.'

We have before referred to the five crosses
surrounding the table at the high altar, and it
may not be considered altogether out of place if
we refer shortly to the changes made in that
great emblem of salvation—the crucifix—in
order to show how ready the Roman Church is to
adapt itself, in matters of even small moment, to
the changes which are taking place in the world
at large and in the spirit of the age. It may
surprise many to hear that the crucifix was not
known until the fifth century. In the sixth the

figure of our Saviour was first attached. In the eleventh the figure was completely clothed. In the twelfth the robe was shortened and the sleeves made to terminate at the elbows. In the thirteenth the robe was exchanged for a cloth girded round the loins; while in the fifteenth century the present configuration of the crucifix was first inaugurated.

The splendour of conventual churches has been most plausibly explained in the announcement that 'personal expense or secular indulgence was culpable in a monk, but what was expended in ornamenting the church was to the glorification of God and the Blessed Virgin.'

The Church exhibited in its primeval glory the utmost magnificence of external ritual—those grand displays in which the Catholicism of Rome, like the paganism it embodied, ever luxuriates. When the monks, clad in their white robes and black hoods which formed the costume of their devotions, passed in pompous procession, chanting solemnly psalms of dole, the fragrant incense in the silver thuribles percolating its innocuous essences around the blazoned altar, brightly illuminated by the

c

flames of many tall candles, and the full, broad
swelling harmony of the great organ filling
the vast interior, when—

> ' Such was the winged music's downy flight
> That echo silent was from exquisite delight.'

the effect, it can well be imagined, was above
all things grand. It would be one of those
impressive scenes wherein the still small voice
within would enforce—' Bow the knee and
mutter, God's will be done.' Doubtless, in those
days, in the height of its glory, the sensuous
religion that first consecrated the glorious
monastic church, haunted still its noble aisles
and revered shrines, hovered ever in each
sumptuous chapel, glided persistently through
the gloom of pillar and arch, and would not
have speeded away until eternity itself, had
Vandalism not swept away the superb and time
honoured sanctuaries.

Had monachism been spared, the very dust
of its conventual churches would have been
purple with the ashes of princes and the great
ones of earth. Their very ruins might have
still been one of the proudest boasts of

England's ecclesiastical architecture, a monument of a dead world's adoration, while

> ' Each ivied arch and pillar lone,
> Pleaded haughtily for glories gone.'

But all has fled. The scorching blast of ruthless Vandalism has passed over its surface, and not even a broken carving, in most places, remains to speak of the chaste beauties and solemn glories that have been. All are gone—the noble church, those rare embellishments, those exquisite monuments, the luminous altar, those majestic ceremonials, and those gorgeous accompaniments. It has been truthfully written *in memoriam*, of the monasteries that—' the hymn was no more to be chanted in the Lady's chapel, and the candles were no more to be lit on the high altar, and the gate of the poor was to be closed for ever, and the wanderer was no more to find a home.' Gone, all gone.—So passed away the beautiful, the magnificent, the rich, the powerful.

> ' Monastic arches, silent cloisters lone
> And ruin'd cells, ye know what loving is.'

Gone are your chill, cold naves, your pavements stone,
Which burning lips did faint o'er when they kiss.

.   .   .   .   .

With your baptismal waters bathe their face,
  Tell them a moment how their knees must wear
The cold sepulchral stones, before the grace
  Of loving as you loved, they hope to share.
Vast was the love, which from your chalices,
  Mysterious monks, with a full heart ye drew,
  Ye loved with ardent souls!   Oh happy lot for you!'

In this general commentary of the monks and
their monasteries it may be both useful and
interesting to refer particularly to the custom
of giving lectures while the principal meal of
the day was in progress.   Generally in one
corner of the common hall where the mid-day
meal was celebrated, and commanding a full
view of all who were partakers of the repast,
was a stone desk or pulpit, from which a
regularly deputed monk, called the lecturer,
read selected passages of Scripture, with a
running commentary thereon, or a homily of
St Chrysostom or other saint; or the Roman
martyrology, that is, the notice of the saint for
the day; or selections from the lives of the
saints, or. as was more commonly the case, some

of those undiscerning legends which too aptly
fed the superstition, and deadened the genuine
soul piety of a dark and gloomy age. This duty
was ordered and strictly enforced, so that, while
the body was being refitted, the spirit too might
have its food. Some of the apologies invented
by the Dominican preachers in their sermons or
lectures were so ingenuous, that we venture to
incur reproach by inserting two as samples.

One is as follows—'A certain scholar in the
University of Bologna, of no good repute, either
for his morals or his manners, found himself
once (it might have been in a dream) in a
certain meadow not far from the city, and there
came on a terrible storm, and he fled for refuge
until he came to a house, where, finding the
door shut, he knocked and entreated shelter.
A voice from within answered: "I am Justice,
I dwell here, and this house is mine, but as thou
art not just, thou canst not enter in." The
young man turned away sorrowfully, and
proceeding further, the rain and the storm
beating upon him, he came to another house,
and again he knocked and entreated shelter. A
voice from within replied: "I am Truth, I dwell

here, and this house is mine, but as thou lovest not truth thou canst not enter here." And further on he came to another house and again besought to enter. A voice from within said: "I am Peace, I dwell here, and this house is mine, but as there is no peace for the wicked and those who fear not God, thou canst not enter here." Then he went on further being much afflicted and mortified, and he came to another door and knocked timidly. A voice from within answered: "I am Mercy, I dwell here, and this house is mine, and if thou wouldst escape from this fearful tempest repair quickly to the dwelling of the Brethren of St Dominick, that is the only asylum for those who are truly penitent." And the scholar failed not to do as this vision had commanded. He took the habit of the order and lived henceforth an example of every virtue.'

The apologue runs after this fashion :—' It is related in the apocryphal Gospel of Nicodemus, that when Adam fell sick, he sent his son Seth to the gate of the terrestrial Paradise to ask the angel in charge thereof for some drops of the oil of mercy, distilled from the tree of life, to

cure him of disease, but the angel answered that
he could not receive this healing oil until 5500
years had passed away. He gave him, however,
a branch of the tree, which was planted upon
Adam's grave. In after ages the branch grew
into a tree, which flourished and waxed exceed-
ing fair, for Adam was buried in Mount
Lebanon, not very far from the place near
Damascus, whence the red earth came, out of
which his body was formed by the Great
Creator. When Balkis, Queen of Abyssinia,
came to visit Solomon the king, she worshipped
this tree, for she prophecied that thereon
should the Saviour of the world be crucified,
and that from that time the kingdom of the
Jews should cease. Upon hearing this, Solomon
commanded that the tree should be cut down
and buried in a certain place in Jerusalem, where
afterwards was dug the pool of Bethseda, and
where the angel who had charge of the mysterious tree troubled the waters at certain seasons,
whereupon those who first dipped into them
were cured of their ailments whatsoever they
were. As the dread time of the Passion of the
Saviour approached, the sacred timber floated

up to the surface of the water. It was at once
secured and out of it the Jews made the upright
part of the cross, the transverse beam being
made of cypress, the piece on which His feet
rested, of palm, and that on which the super-
scription was written, of olive.'

We sum up this general disquisition upon the
birth, growth, and worldly condition of the
Monks and Monasteries of old, by asserting
from the evidences at command, that in those
iron ages, when with rope and faggot, fire and
sword, the virulent piety of even good men
sought to enforce the precepts of Him whose
advent was proclaimed in the angelic hymn of
'Peace on earth and good-will towards men,' the
London houses were, taken as a whole, the best
ordered in England. The discipline was honest
and careful, the charities were profuse, the
hospitality without stain, and their popularity
historically notorious. Whatever we may feel
disposed to think of the pious harlotry of
monachism, and the absurd and childish
functions with which it was enveloped, we may
yet be just to that section of 'The Monks of
Old,' who for so many centuries lived in the

heart of ancient London, and believe that they, at least, were true to their vows and honest in their duties, so far at least as they were capable of understanding the vows they adopted, or of comprehending what duty meant.

Part Second

Commentary on the Monks
of Old

SECTION I

INTRODUCTION

———

WHEN our readers consider how notable was the fundamental character of the many great and beneficent monastic establishments in this country, how vast was their action, how immense the benefits they unitedly bestowed and how deep the ingratitude which at last annihilated them, it will not be thought a work of super-erogation our giving the following analytical account of the habits and duties of the monks of old and of their homes within the metro-politan area. When the impartial reader reflects that the position in the social and political world at one time occupied by the great Benedictine order was that of one of the greatest institutions in Christendom, he will not think these particulars altogether out of place or wholly objectless.

The subject embraces too vast a field to launch into anything like diffuseness—for it is one that belongs not only to the past but to all time. The links by which it is connected with history, remote in the future or far distant in the past, are numerous and manifest. When we look at maps of England as she was in the Middle Ages, the eye encounters in every county and in numberless localities the names of Hermitages, Chapterhouses, Priories, Convents and Abbeys that were at one time so many monastic colonies and which have since bequeathed titles to buildings, districts and even towns, combined in many instances with some more substantial evidences in the form of picturesque and graceful ruins—the ivy-covered chroniclers of ages flown—the dust and ashes of a glorious feudalism.

SECTION II

THEIR RISE AND PROGRESS

OF the first birth of Monachism, it is not easy to write with anything like certainty. It is, however, authenticated that among the ancient Druids, large collegiate institutions existed before the time when on Stonehenge, 'Solemn Druids hymn'd unwritten rhyme.' A society styling itself 'Asceticks,' was formed as early as the second century, the members of which were fired with the ill-judged ambition of imitating the heathen philosophers.* Next in succession, it would appear, arose the Societies of Platonists and Pythagoreans, all seeking the intellectual luxury which was cultivated by elegant retirement. The Crusades, it has been urged, were religious associations organised for martial pilgrimages on an enormous scale. The introduction, however, of Monachism into Eng-

* Fosbrooke's British Monachism.

land, is with somewhat more certainty ascribed
to the fourth century, when the Egyptian Rule,
according to the institutes of Pachomius, was
professed. The first Anglo-Saxon monasteries,
however, were mere convents of secular clerks,
which, like those scattered over the rest of the
wide world, obeyed no uniform code of rules,
but adopted methods of living and working self-
prescribed. This mobilised style of organisation
continued until the ninth century, when general
rules for their future government were ordained
by the head establishments of the several orders,
and when too, for the first time cloisters were
introduced into their dwellings, and became the
favourite resorts of the thoughtful recluse.

Austere principles as to the obligations of
evangelical poverty were inculcated by the
numerous sectaries of that early age, and were,
we are assured,* eagerly received by the people,
previously much alienated from an established
hierarchy. No means appeared so efficacious to
counteract the evils weighing upon them as the
institution of religious societies, strictly debarred
from the insidious temptations of wealth. To

---

* Hallam's Middle Ages, vol. 2, p. 5.

carry into effect this principle, the great
Mendicant Orders had been some time previously
founded throughout the Continent, who were
incapable by the rules of their foundations, of
possessing real property, and who were for the
most part maintained by alms and devout remun-
erations. Their distinctive precept was,—'*Sub-
levanem pauperis sit abstinentia jejunantis*,' or,
the abstinence of him that fasts ought to be a
relief for the poor. Of these, as already shewn,
the two most celebrated and popular were those
formed by St Dominic and St Francis of Assisi,
both subsequently established by the authority
of Pope Honorius the Third in 1216 and 1223.

These latter orders were those which after the
induction of monachism into this country
became the most popular, the most powerful
and most familiarly known in the metropolis
and elsewhere as the Black Friars and the Grey
Friars.

The veneration once so generally exhibited
for these religious institutions must have been
most reasonably enhanced what time they were
treated as sanctuaries, as green spots of peace and
shelter amid a wilderness of tyranny, wrong and

D

desolating violence, as havens of refuge for the persecuted and enfeebled. These privileges formed certainly their fairest attractions and strongest recommendations with the English people in those primitive days.

The Religious Orders may be classed under the four following principal categories:—

First.—The Monks, properly so called, who comprised the sects of St Basil and St Benedict, with all their offshoots, the Cluny, the Carmadules, the Chartreux, the Cistercians, the Celestines, the Fontevrault and the Grandmont, all anterior to the thirteenth century.

Second.—The Regular Canons, who followed the Rule of St Augustine and who neither gained great distinction nor rendered eminent services, but to whom notwithstanding were attracted two illustrious orders, namely, that of Premontre and that of La Merci, for the redemption of captives.

Third.—The Brothers (*Fratri*) or religious mendicants, who comprehended the Dominicans, the Franciscans,—with all their branches of Conventuals Observantins, Recollets and Capucins—the Carmelites, the Augustines, the

Servites, the Minimes and generally all the brotherhoods organised between the thirteenth and sixteenth centuries.

Fourth.—The Regular Clerks, a sect comprising exclusively the orders created since the sixteenth century, such as those of the Jesuits, the Theatins, the Barnabites, etc.

The Lazarists, the Oratorians and the Eudistes were merely sects like the Sulpiciens, only secular priests united in a congregation.

———

SECTION III

THEIR MANNERS AND CUSTOMS

THE grand doctrine practised in their most remote ancientry by 'the monks of old' was— the extenuation of the sluggish body by hunger, thrist and other mortifications. The great ruling principle among them in times less remote was that, 'purity of mind and body are presumed to result through insulation from the world and through humility and abstinence. Self-command and cheerfulness were deemed easy acquisitions. The profession of monachism was, however, considered by all sects and all grades, as a kind of second baptism. We can readily understand that such precepts as these recommended the monkish system very strongly to the Anglo-Saxons, among whom it is well known that virtue consisted in abstinence from gluttony and pleasure.

In the infancy of monachism, the diet of the monks was of the simplest kind, consisting of bread, pulse and herbs, accompanied by water and sometimes milk, but never wine. Their dress too was then in keeping with their simple habits. Many clothed themselves with the bristles of camels, while softer garments were considered a criminal acquisition. They seldom left their cells in those days unless to assemble in the church for prayer or for manual labour. All things then too were held in common. These ancient monks worked hard in the early arts, in manufactures and even in road making.* Their

* Anglia Sacra, vol. ii. pp. 629, 655 and 662.

education consisted of psalmody, music, accounts, grammar, writing, turning and carpentry. Subsequently every known art and labour was practised among them.

In its ancientry Monachism was also upheld by women, being in many recorded instances sought by them as a refuge, long before convents for nuns were founded. They of course fled to these havens in male attire, and as one among many at hand, we quote the following recorded example.—The legend of St Margaret sets forth that — 'Soon after marriage she kept her from the companye of her husbonde and at midnight she commended her to God and cut off her hayre and cladde her in the habyte of a man, and fledde fro thens to a monastery of monkes.'*

In later times the duties of the monks resolved themselves into the following general code. They were to pray and weep for their faults, to subdue their flesh, to watch and abstain from pleasures, to bridle their tongues and shut their ears to vanities, to guard their eyes and to keep their feet from wandering, to

* Golden Legend, fol. 180.

labour with their hands, exult with their lips and rejoice at heart in the praises of God, to bare the head, bow down and bend the knees at the feet of the crucifix, to obey readily, never contradicting their superiors, to serve willingly and assist speedily the sick brethren, to throw off the cares of the world and attend to celestial concerns with their utmost endeavours, and not to be overcome by the arts of Satan, but to do everything with prudence.*

Silence was one of the principally enforced characteristics of a monk, for its observance was supposed to prevent a multitude of sins, and therefore, it was only at certain intervals and in certain privileged places conversation was permitted. Their eyes too, after the custom of the Pharisees, were generally fixed on the ground, while their heads were bent lowly downwards. They therefore were enforced to do by signs what words would have accomplished, and these signs were displayed after a well-constructed rule and were taught to the novices like the alphabet. But even signs were forbidden, when at certain seasons silence was strictly enjoined,

* Fosbrooke's British Monachism.

for translating from the *Monita Moralia* of
Nizell de Wireker, we find the lines—

> ' As statues still if ordered so, abide,
> Nor seek by *signs* the speech that is denied.'

The rule of duties for daily observance was
thus apportioned—The hour of rising proclaimed
by the dormitory bell, was on week days at
2 A.M., and on Sundays and festivals at 1 A.M.
The monks then proceeded to the church, to
rehearse the offices of *Matins* and *Lauds* until
4 A.M. They then employed themselves till
5 A.M., in prayerful solitude or private contemplation in church, or in perusing some sacred
work in the cloisters. They again attended in
the church at 6 A.M., to join in the Service of
Prime. After which was held for half-an-hour,
a chapter of faults. Then for one hour, were
performed all the many manual duties and
exercises allotted to each. These were deserted
at the sound of the church bell, which summoned the monks at 9 A.M., to the service of
Tierce, Shortly after *High Mass* followed, and
subsequently, after a short interval of study,

prayer or renewed contemplation, was given at 12 noon the service of *Sext*. They then adjourned to the *Refectory*, where the principal meal of the day was solemnly discussed. In winter, *Nones* followed at 2 P.M., in summer at 3 P.M. After that service they returned for an hour-and-a-half to their manual avocations, leaving off when the bell summoned them to church to pray for the *King*. At 4 P.M. *Vespers* was performed, and at 5 P.M. they again resorted to the *Refectory* for a slight repast. Afterwards they had an hour-and-a-half to pass either in the *Cloister*, *Close Garden*, or *Common Hall*, after which, at 7 P.M., they joined in the last service, *Completorium* or *Complins*, which ended with the following versicle from the Psalmist, 'Set a watch, O Lord, before my mouth, and keep the door of my lips,' and then at 8 P.M. retired to the *Dormitory*.

On the above severe mode of life, the poet Crashaw comments thus,—

> ' A hasty portion of prescribed sleep,
> Obedient slumbers that can wake and weep,
> And sing, and sigh, and work, and sleep again,
> Still rolling a round sphere of still returning pain,

Hands full of hearty labours, pains that pay
And prize themselves, do much more they may,
And work for work, not wages, let to-morrow's
New drops wash off the sweat of their day's sorrows,
A long and daily-dying life which breathes
A respiration of reviving deaths.'

Like the feudal nobles, and indeed previously
to them, the monks possessed that taste for the
picturesque—Nature, in her wild, abrupt and
varied aspect, which prevailed throughout the
middle ages. They discovered and enjoyed all
the poetry of nature. They appeared to be
impressed with the same delicate and profound
appreciation of rural scenery, which had
dictated to Virgil and Dante so many immortal
verses. In every instance where trace can be
found of their settlements in provincial districts,
either at home or abroad, we find that the
fairest corners of the very fairest localities were
selected by them for the erection of their conventual homes, and for the seclusion of their
persons, while enjoying, as they were wont to
believe, a medicine which was for eternity as
well as for life.

We have, in the course of our previous de-
scriptions, sufficiently rehearsed the sumptuous

splendour that prevailed in the churches of these 'monks of old.' Little else we are told was to be discerned in them but marble, porphyry, jasperstone, and the most exquisite paintings and statuary. The crosses, the candlesticks, the vessels for the Eucharist, the lamps, the censers, the cases for the reliquaries, and the other adornments of the altar, were all for the most part of gold or silver, beset with precious stones, while at the same time they were almost infinite in number and value, affording collectively a lustre, whose beauty ravished the soul through the organs of the sight. It would be well nigh a hopeless task to enumerate the number of limners or painters constantly at work in gloriously adorning these old monastic temples, nor would it be advantaging to recite the festal services and sacraments of the old monastic *regime*, for the majority of them are still celebrated by the Church of Rome, but all of which then controlled the adoring worshipper to exclaim, ' *Quam augusta est Domus Dei!* ' or, How glorious is the House of God!

Forasmuch as throughout the Middle Ages,

inns having any pretension to comfort or good
entertainment were few and far between, the
monasteries were generally patronised by the
roving and well-to-do class of the population,
as the best conditioned resting places. Among
the virtues of 'the monks of old' hospitality
was very prominent, although the custom invariably was to limit the extent of their
hospitality to three days, and during that period
treating their guests on a sliding scale adapted
to their rank or quality.

They were not only the greatest patrons and
encouragers of art, but included among their
own phalanx some of the most memorable
artists of that or any age. But as a proof, how
even in minor matters these cenobites fostered
general industry, we have merely to repeat what
is freely acknowledged, that they were the best
and indeed the only scientific gardeners and
husbandmen. Even in the present day the
Capuchins are famed among the best horticul-
turists of Europe. The gardens of most of the
larger monasteries, with their fair grassplots,
fine parterres of flowers, pleasant fountains,
and great avenues of trees and shrubs, were not

unworthy to rank as first-class horticultural exhibitions.

That superstition of the rankest kind prevailed amid the army of cenobites, none can or will gainsay, and most notably may be mentioned the very common custom of attributing release from danger, recovery from illness, and escape from death or misfortune to the intervention of the saint to whose image or statue the afflicted had previously made vows. As a sequel to this belief it so happened that, after renewal to health or life the devotee proceeded to commemorate the occasion by having the evidence of it recorded in the corner of some picture with the letters P.G.R. thereunder written, signifying, '*Pro Gratia Ricevata*,'—for grace received. These vowed pictures, many in number, were to be found hung up in the churches of every monastery.

These monks devoutly believed in miracles and upheld the spirit of prophecy. The miracles and prophecies enacted by their chief female' saints were announced to have been recorded by themselves, including such holy personages as St Bridget, St Mechilda, St Catharine of

Sienna, St Gertrude and a numerous phalanx. These prophetesses were held in extreme veneration, and with the want of such saintly support were the early Protestants taunted by the oft repeated sentence,—'*Apud quos cessavit propheta.*' To recite the record of examples propounded by them were to fill volumes instead of pages. But in this place, as another evidence of their facile superstition we must record that many of them believed in privileged altars, that is to say, altars to which the Popes had affixed certain unusual indulgences, such as, if only one mass was said at them for a soul in purgatory, that soul was infallibly delivered therefrom.

The errors which they admitted still pertained to their humanity in their cloistral retirement, and which perchance were the ones they most frequently suffered under were after this sort, that sometimes by frailty they broke the strongly enjoined observance of silence, that they walked with too much haste and precipitancy, that they cast about them looks of too enquiring a nature, that they were occasionally slovenly in their habits, that they preferred vocal to mental prayer, that they were oft times too much

pleased with the taste of heavenly music or that
they were prone to be too heavy and cast down
under sufferings.   Limiting thus haughtily and
proudly their errors of omission and commis-
sion has brought upon them the condemnation of
the Pharisee—' *Non sunt sicut cæteri hominum,*'
or, they are not like other men.

While none were more stoical in their discourses on death than ' the monks of old,' we
are   assured   few   were   more   cowardly   or
frightened than they, when, their hour having
come, they had to face the Dim Unknown.

We have already stated that miracles were
upheld by them.   To that statement we now
add that polytheism existed among them, while
empiricism was used as an influence by them.
They   believed   profoundly   in   the   spirit   of
Divination, often consulted some augury, and
included, in certain houses, among their officials
men known as *imaginarii* or sorcerers.

They wore diurnal and nocturnal shoes.   In
what the difference consisted we cannot trace.
They   served   weekly   and   by   turns   in   the
different offices connected with their monastery.
When taking part in the various daily or festal

offices of the church, they always proceeded to
the *Vestiary* to assume their vestments.

The monks were often engaged in civil and
other public avocations. They were frequently
selected as ambassadors and special commis-
sioners.* They were, too, throughout the dark
ages, the great loanmongers of the age.†

They would salute each other with a '*Bene-
dicite*,' receiving the reply, '*Dominus*,' while in
their services, meetings and lectures they used
the tongue which Tully chastely spoke and
Maro sweetly sung.

The whole of the religious orders were bound
by oaths similar to those which, some years
since, created difficulty in Oxford. They were
sworn to divulge nothing which might prejudice
the interest of their houses. Even the lay
brethren, or serving men, were enforced to take
the oath of fidelity not to reveal the secrets of
their conventual.

Each large monastery had a number of
serving men to aid in carrying out the orders
of the officials. At Tewkesbury, for instance, it

---

* Fosbrooke's British Monachism.
† Toulmin's Taunton, p. 8.

was ascertained after the dissolution, there were
no fewer than 144*   While every monastery
had its titular Saint and every Saint his legend.

Time was always allowed the monks for daily
study, and among the ancient MSS. in their
libraries, and to which they, one and all, had
access, were copies of the works of Livy,
Sallust, Lucan, Virgil, Claudian, etc.

Festivals were always great occasions among
them, and with which, it is said, *Saturnalia*
was closely engrafted.   These feasts represented
those days in the year which were to be more
religiously observed than the rest, in honour
either of the Virgin, the Rosary, the Holy
Week, some mystery of the Gospel, some Saint,
or some special blessing.   On these occasions,
designated by monks, '*Pontificals*,' a great show
of the riches and grandeur of each house was
made.   Among the outside feasts were those
of Advent, Shrovetide, Christmas, Ascension,
Pentecost, the Octave of the Holy Sacra-
ment, etc.

The Dominicans preached most frequently on
the rosary, the Carmelites on the scapulary, the

* Dyde's History of Tewkesbury, p. 146.

Franciscans on the rope of St Francis, and the Socolanti on St Anthony.

The Dominicans used to make a procession in honour of the rosary every first Sunday in the month, the Carmelites one in honour of the scapulary on the second, and the Franciscans one in honour of the rope of St Francis on the third.

The Superiors of these sects almost invariably suffered their preaching brethren to do what they thought fit in the exercise of their vocation, or go where they wished in favour of their invention—as they used to term it. They consequently indulged in all manner of extravagances—in style, in declamation, in quotation and in action. They made use of Scripture as an ally, without preaching on it or in explanation of any selected portion. They contented themselves by referring to it with the preface, 'as it is written,' or, 'according to the oracle of the Holy Spirit,' or, 'as it is set down in the sacred text.' Sometimes when referring to the ever-increasing list of the fathers of the Church, they would have the vanity to exclaim, 'St Austin, or St Jerome, or St Ambrose had the same thought with me when he said,' etc.

E

These preaching friars each pursued a different line of character, befitting his own peculiar powers and capacity and in many respects simulated actors in their elocution and movements. There were those who preached stoically and emphatically, albeit in a voice of thunder, deep and terrible things, such as Death, the Last Judgment, Purgatory and Hell, and with every accessory requisite for a single actor, to represent it as the deepest tragedy. There were others who held curious ideas and expounded them, and these were named *Dotti* or *Virtuosi* and were the most patronised and esteemed. Others again, there were who represented the buffoons or comic characters, and these were the most sought after by the common people. The sermons of these latter consisted of idle tales and drollery of speech and action. As their pulpits were made purposely large, they forcibly enunciated many of their mountebank notions by assuming the characters they were making mention of, and going through their supposed comic action. They thumped their pulpits with feet and hands, pulled their beards and hair, laughed and cried aloud, rolled their eyes wildly in their heads and put themselves into a hundred ridiculous postures. There was yet another class who, like the Jesuits, had a poetical style and commonly quoted passages drawn from profane authors, such as Cicero, Virgil, Horace, Martial, and even from the comedies of Terence as well as from Ovid's '*De Arte Amandi.*' These last were the best elocutionists.

The whole of these preaching monks commenced their sermons, for the most part, with the angelical salutation, '*Ave Maria.*' Then they quoted their text, which was generally confined to the name of some place, or to two or three words, but which never embodied an entire passage. The discourse itself was generally divided into two parts, and during the interval, alms for the poor were collected from the audience.

Many preached in public open resorts, such as in the noon of market-tide, or in the midst of the hurly-burly of a fair, in furtherance of the oracle set forth in the first chapter of Proverbs—'Wisdom cries in the public places.'

SECTION IV

THEIR OFFICES AND OFFICERS

The Church.—Of this we have already written pretty fully. Let us, however, be permitted to enlarge upon what has already been detailed, by stating further, that upon every edifice of importance, the most famous architects exhausted their skill, the most renowned painters devoted the utmost elaboration of their art, the most profuse gilders or decorators laid their first gold or colours, while the most distant quarries of earth rendered up their choicest marbles, jaspers and porphyries. The *Altar* was the golden calf, the brazen serpent, and the god of monastic idolatry, on which was consummated splendour, pomp, and gorgeousness. It was surmounted by numerous and rare '*reliquaries.*' It was illuminated by innumerable candles. It was perfumed by ever smoking golden *thuribles.*

While its authentic specialty, the five lustrous crosses, gleamed high amid the sumptuous surroundings. Close beside the church stood the church-yard called the *Polyandrium*.

The Chapter House—This room or hall generally had three rows of stone seats one above the other, a reading desk and settle, a place enclosed called the '*Judgment*' in the centre, a seat for the *Abbot* or *Prior* higher than the benches, and a large crucifix directly behind the desk. At 9 A.M. the monks assembled here, and being seated, the proceedings were commenced by a short religious service. Then followed the reading of the sentence of the *Rule* from the desk, after which the *Table* was read and anyone who had omitted a prescribed *Office* solicited pardon. Then the commemoration for the dead—the *Martyrology* and *Obituary*—was recited and always brought to a close by the '*Requiescat in pace*.' To this succeeded the voluntary confessions, and after that came the accusation or *Clamatio* of offenders. The monastic courts, taking cognizance of everything within the precincts or limits of the conventual property, were held here. The sway of these courts

reached the tenants of the monks and all those
seculars who were in any way subservient to
them, together with those strangers who committed crimes upon the lands pertaining to the
monastery. In some cases an appeal was
allowed to the king, but to the king only.

The Refectory.—From this chamber there was
an entrance direct to the *Kitchen* and another
to the *Cellar*. Closely adjoining was the *Lava-
tory*, while in a corner stood a small recess or
closet, called the *Almery* and containing the
Grace-cup. Fires were lighted herein from All
Hallows Day till Good Friday. The utmost
number of meals, even among those cenobites
who were most profuse in their good cheer, were
the following—morning repast, drinking after
Nones, dinner, collation, and late supper, called
consolatio. A small bell, termed the *cymbalum*,
was struck in the *Cloister* to summon to meals.
The upper table, forming the cross, was generally
slightly raised. The novices dined after the
monks, and the servants or lay brethren after
the novices. There was a pulpit in this apart-
ment for the reading of appointed portions of
the Scriptures or other works during meal time.

When this was brought to a close the Prior rose, exclaiming '*Tu autem*,' the lecturer replying, '*Deo gratias*.' The monks thereupon retired from table, two and two, singing the *Miserere*.

The Dormitory—was called very frequently the *Dortor*. In the larger monasteries, each monk had a little chamber or wooden compartment to himself. The hours of rising were as before stated, at 2 A.M. on week days and 1 A.M. on Sundays or festivals. The hour for retiring to rest generally 9 P.M. The *Meridians* or hour of rest in the middle of the day began on Palm Sunday and continued to the Ides of September.

The Cloister.—This was originated for meditation as well as exercise during bad weather. Most of the principal offices could be reached by passing through it. There were seats there for those to sit upon who had to study. The processions, so full of pomp and splendour, were always formed here before proceeding into the church.

The Scriptorium.—This was sometimes called the *Domus Antiquariorum*, but was simply the writing room. The *Abbot, Prior, Sub-Prior* and

Precentor, were only admitted into this treasury of beautiful missals and other MSS. books of divine offices of the early Church. A certain selected number of the brotherhood, surnamed the *Antiquarii* were here continually employed in copying or writing up the monastic daily history. Under these, *Antiquarii*, who were men of superior stamp and education, worked the *Scriptores* or *Librarii*—copyists. The writing was generally good and clear. The character of the lettering nearly approached the present Roman. The first painters of the age were frequently engaged in illuminating the MSS. Gold and azure were the principal and favourite colours employed. Under these painters, performed their pupils or Limners.* Paper books cannot be traced beyond the tenth century, while printing and engraving were discovered about 1460. But *Scribes* and *Limners* continued occupied on MSS. for fully a century longer, indeed until the dissolution of the monasteries swept them away,† Bookbinding was occasionally very grand.

° Dugdale's Monasticon.
† Fosbrooke's British Monachism.

The Library and Museum.—These together
with all the *Muniments* of the Monastery, were
under the carè of the *Chantor*. They were
generally well furnished with rarities and
curiosities. The books being mostly MSS.,
were rolled and placed in painted presses or
almeries. Many of these were of the most
bizarre kind, but prominent among them
always stood the family narrative of the
Monastery, edited by their classical *actuarius*
or historiographer. Among them were, however, invariably good copies of the old Greek
and Latin masters.

The Guest Hall was variously denominated
the *Hospice*, the *Hostrey* or the *Hostelry*. It
had passages of communication with the *Kitchen*, *Buttery* and *Cellar*. It was generally very
roomy and handsome, and was sometimes, in
consequence, called the *Palatium*. Connected
with it were numerous bed-chambers, and also
a sort of ante-room, termed the *Pro-aula*, the
Salutarium or the greeting house. Visitors
were permitted to stay two days and two nights,
but were to depart on the third, meanwhile in all
respects conforming to the rules and attending

the services selected. The attention shown and the accommodation afforded, was in accord with the rank of the visitor. In fact great flatteries and much unseemly adulation were at times exhibited to high personages. The *Hosteler* met the visitors and after the *Benedicte* saluted them with 'the kiss of peace.'

The Infirmary.—This department was frequently crowded with every necessity, for it was open to strangers as well as to the brethren. It was strewed with rushes or clean hay and straw. It had a great table for the generous diet, always shown, to be served upon, a chapel annexed, where special daily services were performed and a stone of unction, whereon the dying were washed and clothed in their last swathements. Several chambers, conveniently fitted for the sick, led off from it. The *Prior*, *Sub-Prior* or *Kitchener* were bound each day, before *Prime*, to visit it, and carefully inspect all in connection with it. It was the duty of the *Infirmarer* to administer the communion to the dying.

The Locutory or Parlour.—Of these there were generally two in each monastery, one for the visitors, closely adjoining the Guest Hall, another for the monks for conversation called the *auditorium*. But no cloistral devotee could enter the latter without previous summons or license of the *Abbot* or *Prior*. Here merchants were received and were wont to expose their goods or samples.

The Almonry or Alms-house was an important appendage to all monasteries, which were indeed, throughout the Middle Ages, the great fountains of charitable aid. It was generally a large stone building erected near the church, wherein all kinds of relief were freely and amply granted to the suffering and indigent poor. The alms were, for the most part, distributed on fixed days, but no one was ever sent empty away. The tenth part of all monastic revenues was set apart for this department.

The Common-house.—This was the only place of common resort for the monks, where they were allowed to meet at certain hours and converse. It was a large and comfortable room, well warmed in winter. It had a garden and bowling alley attached to it, for the use of the novices, who chiefly resorted to it. Here the rod of discipline was hung up over the fireplace.

The Misericord was a large plain ·furnished hall, where the monks assembled during *Misericorde*—certain indulgences or exonerations from the duties of the cloister or choir, granted to conventuals alternately, and lasting a week at a time. They were then and here allowed to converse at ease and without any restraint.

The Kitchen.—A much more extensive office than modern ones in private houses. The culinary apparatus was very large and numerous. Attached to it were several storehouses for keeping cured fish, salted provisions, vegetables, etc.

The Bakehouse.—Herein was first manufactured the *Host*, of unfermented bread; then the *Oblatæ*, or unconsecrated cakes, which were afterwards blessed on the altar; then the *Eulogiæ*, or consecrated loaves, sent out to friends or given to visitors in token of *Communion*; and finally the daily bread.

The Mint.—The money coined herein was by license. A master thereof was appointed by the *Abbot* or *Prior*. The stamps for coining were granted as a privilege.

The Exchequer.—This was a small chamber or

counting house, with a square table in it,
curiously marked for calculation—a long process
in those days of simple arithmetic.

The Cells.—These were either for recreation or
punishment, and were invariably detached from
the monastery proper. Two or three monks
together would frequent the former.

The Granges.—The farms and park lands
attached or pertaining to the estate of the
monastery were so called.

The Sanctuary.—In some cases this included
a large area, as in Westminster, Blackfriars,
St Bartholomew's, etc.; but most frequently only
a small and selected spot within the church.
Living in Sanctuary by the laity was, for the
most part, very expensive.

The Lying House.—This was a prison. The
Abbot or *Prior* had arbitrary powers of punishment. Monks guilty of felony or adultery were
imprisoned in chains for a year.

The Song School.—This was built generally
within the church, at times in the roof, at others
in the crypt. A master was appointed, who
taught the novices and lay children herein to
sing and play on the organ.

The Vestiary.—This was also situated within the church and adjoined the altar. There were often double *Vestiaries*. Here were deposited the garments and *Cimelia* of the church. It consisted for the most part of a series of stone closets.

To these various offices must be added the *Garden*, wherein the monks laboured or sought recreation. The *Fratry*, adorned with curious painted imageries, the *Stable*, the *Dove-cot*, the *Cow-house*, etc.

So much for the several distinctive offices in the small world of a monastery. Now for the officers, a fairly numerous host.

The Abbot.—As heads or rulers of a monastic home, *Abbots* and *Priors*, except in cases of cathedrals, were usually considered synonymous. Their duties and obligations were similar. He was elected after various modes and in accordance with the *Chartulary* of the convent. After election he went through the ceremonials of *Benediction* and *Induction*. He had to celebrate *Mass* and dine in the *Refectory*, only on festival occasions. He alone could reprove or accuse a monk. He attended in the *Cloister*

every morning to hear what the monks had to
say. He gave his orders direct to the *Sub-Prior*.
He could at will attend any service or collation,
could celebrate private mass, assisted solely by
and in the presence only of his chaplains, who
were called *Monitores*, because they informed
him of all that took place, and of whom he
sometimes had as many as six. He had power
to consecrate churches, had his secret *Oratory*, a
separate table, and sat every Sunday in the
cloister to hear confessions. All had to incline
to him as he passed, while none could sit in his
presence. He attended the bedside of all dying
within the convent. He could not, however,
absent himself for more than three days, and
required the consent of the *Chapter* to go
abroad. He had two assistants in his duties,
who were respectively designated the *Proctor*
and the *Curiarius*. His principal duty was to
set a lofty example in his observation of the
Rule.

The Prior.—In those instances where there
was an *Abbot* the extra-judicial duties of the
Prior were as undermentioned. But if there
was no *Abbot* then these duties were divided

between the *Prior* and *Sub-Prior.*—Next to
the *Abbot,* he was head of the establishment.
He held first place in the *Choir Chapter* and
Refectory, had power to punish and to direct the
rest of the brotherhood, had a chaplain, two
servants, two palfreys, and a baggage horse.
The *Claustral* or *Sub-Prior* was his *Vicar.* He
had chiefly to superintend the *Cloister* and had
the general charge of the establishment. He
had a chamber and sometimes a suite of rooms
called '*lodgings.*' The monks always made
obeisance to him, and he headed the procession
to the *Dormitory* after *Complins.*

The Sub-Prior.—His chamber was close beside the dormitory door, and he was accountable
for the safe durance of all the monks during
sleeping time. He always sat among the monks
at meal time to see order preserved and said
grace thereat. He kept the keys of the *Cloister*
gates, while the infirmary was under his special
care. When the Abbot or Prior, or both, were
absent he had to perform their duties. He was
selected from the general body for his zeal,
devotion and superior attainments.

The Cellarer.—He had care of everything

relating to the dietary of the monks. He had charge of all the vessels in *Kitchen, Refectory* and *Cellar*. He was allowed to be absent from all services except *Matins, Vespers* and *Prime*. He had to wait upon the visitors, the *Minuti* and the monks returning from journeys. In fact he was Commissary-General of the monastery. His chamber was a separate one within the *Dortor*.

The Precentor or Chantor.—He could only be one who had been educated in the monastery from a child. He had the entire supervision of the choral service, and was elected by the *Abbot, Prior* and *Convent*. He taught the monks to sing and read, had an allowance beyond the commons of the house, registered the names of the deceased brethren in the *Martyrology* or obituary, and arranged the processions and order of service at all fasts, and on all festivals. The *Archives* were in his possession, and were delivered by him to the *Almoner* to make out the *Brevia*. Nobody could leave the *Choir* during service without his leave.

The Succentor or Sub-Chantor.—This official was elected at the request and by the choice of

F

the *Chantor*. The keys of the different lockers containing the music, scores, etc., were in his custody, and he entered all missives going from or coming into the monastery. He repeated the answers to the *Chantor* at the different services.

The Kitchener was free from every weekday office except *High Mass*. He sat on the left of the *Prior* at meals, and gave the license to the *Lecturer*, as well as to commence meals. He superintended the wants of the sick, had a horse allowed him, with which to attend markets, etc. He was obliged to be well acquainted with the art of cooking, as he acted as superintendent to the cooks, of whom there were several, all and wholly subject to him. The *vicarius* or herdsman was also under him. He was allowed a companion, who was termed the *Solatium*.

The Sacrist had to perform various duties for the officiating priest, to ring the mass bell, to superintend burials, to distribute the candles for the offices, and furnish wafers for the communicants. He had the custody of the church, the bells, banners, etc. He had a chamber in the *Dortor*, but at night invariably slept in the church. He prepared the *Host* and washed the *Corporals* (the cloths in which the *Host* was wrapped), and the *Ampullæ* (the vessels used to pour the wine into the chalices). He had an attendant called the *Matricularius*, who rang the bells, regulated the *Horologue*, awakened the monks, assisted in sweeping the church, cleaning the lamps, etc.

The Sub-Sacrist.—He was appointed, and performed all the duties required, by the *Sacrist*. He also slept in the church, lighted the lamps on the altar, prepared and fired the incense.

The Seneschal was often a layman of rank, the office being held by fee. He transacted the Abbot or Prior's business with the king, held courts, and had valuable fees and privileges.

The Sub-Seneschal was subject to and appointed by the *Seneschal*, was frequently a layman, was always ready to do the *Convent's* business with the Prior and Cellarer. He had one servant allowed, and received as wages £10 a year.

The Almoner had to provide certain articles for the comfort and convenience of the monastics. Such as mats for kneeling, rods for the chapter, chapel and boys' school, brooms, plates, baskets and other household goods. He had to make out the *Brevia* or annunciation of the deaths of the monks, to find the necessaries for the *Maundy*, to see the gates of the *Locutory* were guarded, had the care of the convent garden, and distributed the alms to the poor. He could go out on the business of the establishment without leave.

The Refectioner.—He distributed the bread and cheese at refection with his own hand, and received the wine whenever it was given out, himself distributing to the monks. He attended to the visitors during meal time, and presided over the distribution of charities to the brethren on certain feasts. He had straw found him, with which he strewed the floor of the *Refectory* where the monks sat. He had to be present at *Matins* and *Primes*, and had under him as a help a somewhat obscure official called the *Pittancer.*

The Chamberlain.—He was to find every requisite for the clothing, bedding, cleanliness and shaving of the monks. He was what may be termed the upholsterer, glazier and clothier of the monastic establishment, as well also, the blacksmith for the stables, and consequently attended fairs to purchase the necessary materials. He provided the baths for general use and employed two helps to attend them. His stores were generally situated in the inner cloister, where he had a *Tailor* constantly at work. He had an ally in the *Sub-Chamberlain* whom he controlled and appointed, and who distributed the clothes, prepared the beds and lighted and extinguished the candles of the Novices.

The Hospitaller or Hosteler.—He presided over the *Hostrey* or guest chambers. Lanterns were found him by the *Chamberlain* and candles by the *Sacrist.* He showed the offices to those strangers who desired to view them and inducted the *Novices* and stranger monks.

The Infirmarer had a separate kitchen and cook for his *Infirmary* and patients, and had to provide all things necessary for his department. He was appointed by the Abbot or Prior with consent of the *Chapter.*

The Bursar or Treasurer had a separate

chamber in or near the *Infirmary*, and an office called the *Exchequer* within the yard, wherein he received the rents of the monastery lands, etc. All the other officials rendered to him their accounts, and he paid all wages and out-goings, etc.

The Lecturer.—He read portions of Scripture or of the lives of the saints, or some old monastic legends, at collation in the *Refectory*. He wore the habit of the professed, and went about lecturing or expounding the canon law to seculars.

The Master of the Novices was chosen by the Prior and had the entire management and instructions of the *Novices*. He was generally an aged man, but was always the most learned and diligent in the convent.

The Janitor or Porter was invariably a man of mature age and unblameable life. He had two meals a day, with beer and certain valuable fees and privileges. He was to be present at the *Chapter, Mass, Vespers* and *Matins*. When the bell tolled for *Complins* at curfew he locked the outer gates and took the keys to the Abbot or Prior. He lay at night in

a little hut or cabin near the gate. He had a
deputy who was never absent when his master
went with messages or to announce visitors.

The Obedientiaries.—These were certain officials
under the Abbot or Prior, who did not generally
bear very good characters, and who were appointed through favour or by purchase.

Among the minor officials, we find the *Master
of the Common-house*, who superintended the
small comforts allowed to the monks, and who
took charge of the office from which he received
his title ; the *Registrarius* or *Cancellarius,* who
attended to the correspondence ; the *Vigilarius*,
who awakened the monks ; the *Actuarius*, who
was the historian of the Monastery ; the *Ex-
plorator*, who was a kind of watchman,
searching the cloisters and precincts after the
monks had retired to the *Dormitory* ; the
Operarius, who was the foreman of the opera-
tives who did the repairs, and who had under
him several artisans ; the *Virgultarius* or
Orcharder, who superintended the harvesting of
the orchards, the storage of the fruit and the
distribution of it ; the *Porcarius*, who attended
to the pig-yard ; the *Granaterius* or keeper of

the garners, who received, had charge of, and distributed all the wheat, barley and malt; the *Ferrier of the House*, who attended to the horses of the guests; the *Lardenarius* or keeper of the larder, together with several bakers, sub-bakers, gardeners, and others.

Of the brethren in general, we have already said so much, that little remains to be written. But it were well here to state that every convent was divided into three grades, forms or divisions, as follows :—

1st. *Sempectæ*, being those who had passed the age of fifty, who were allowed chambers in the infirmary, with a *Junior* for a companion, and a boy to wait upon them. This class passed unrestricted to and fro.

2nd. *The Seniors*, or those who were between the ages of forty and fifty and who were exempt from the offices of the *Almonry*, *Kitchen*, *Cellar* and other mean ones.

3rd. *The Juniors*, who up to the twenty-fourth year of their profession bore all the burthens of the *Choir*, *Cloister* and *Refectory*, and for the next sixteen years were exonerated from the duties of the *Chantries*, *Epistle*, *Gospel* and other similar labours. After the expiration of the last period they undertook the important business of their convent.

To these divisions must be added first the *Novices*, who for two years were only students, acquiring the learning and gaining the bent necessary for the *Professed*, and who, during the *Novitiate*, did not wear the *tonsure* of the monk, and then the *Boys*, who were taught writing, reading and singing, but who were educated not only for the requirements of the conventual *Choir*, but through good will and out of charity to the poor tenants or adherents of the monks.

SECTION V

THEIR MERITS AND DEMERITS

WE have already sufficiently testified on behalf of ' the monks of old,' the fact—that they were the great inventors and foster-nurses of Art,

Literature and Science. That throughout those
ages—misnamed Dark, simply because we know
so little about them—they were the gentle, but
by no means weak, antagonists to tyranny.
That they were the only real working philosophers and philanthropists, doing good in a
practical way everywhere over the broad surface
of the globe.

In the relief of indigence, their most in-
veterate condemners admit they in no way
fell short. But their opponents must go further
than this. They must allow that as architects, as glass painters, as mosaic workers,
as carvers in wood and metal, the monks were
the great precursors of all that has since been
accomplished in Christian Art. This is beyond
dispute. In the monasteries still existing abroad,
may be seen crosses, candlesticks, and reliquaries,
many of splendid workmanship and of the era
of the foundation of the buildings which contain
them, while their mosaics, carvings and paintings
display the state of the arts in the early periods
to which we refer.*

Let those who doubt the charity, humility,

* Curzon's Monasteries of the Levant.

and good sense of the higher orders of 'the monks of old,' peruse as an interesting curiosity the Testament of St Francis, to be found among the Cotton MSS. in the British Museum.

The clerical claim on behalf of the old monasteries was, that the goods of them, were the goods of the poor—'*Bonum pauperum et non regum neque nobilium*,' and certainly, this noble eleemosynary precept appears to have been, for the most part, nobly fulfilled.

Much that has been recorded of the wealth of the monastic bodies needs correction. By far the greater proportion of them at the time of the dissolution, were, on the contrary, poor. The mendicant sectaries, the most numerous in this country, lived as their title implies, by alms and endowments, limited to a degree. There were none truly rich, save the ancient orders of monks such as the Benedictines and Cistercians, while even among them there were monasteries greatly impoverished, especially by the *commende*. Christians of all ranks and times have given, and given much, to these religious institutions, and while they enriched one, they failed not to nourish and raise up others. The munificence of kings assured the existence of many great and noble Abbeys, which served at once for the storing of Archives, the giving of Sanctuary, the holding of Councils and Parliaments, and for the Sepulchre of Dynasties. The treasures of the monks, while so much over-rated, were nevertheless legitimate acquisitions, and were 'the offerings of the faithful, the patrimony of the poor, and the ransom of souls.'

Imperfect the monks certainly were. They were frail men attempting prematurely to clothe themselves in a higher nature. But sacrifice was, undoubtedly, the grand principle of their rule and one which, in England, for near eight centuries was fairly carried out.* Rude ideas, barbarous society, Egyptian superstitions, and the Roman Catholic religion, solve all the errors of monachism.† We may perhaps not unfairly assert that it was an institution founded upon the first principles of religious virtue, wrongly understood and wrongly directed.

Among the gravest accusations from time to time urged against the monks and the system

* Froude's Hist. of England.
† Fosbrooke's British Monachism.

they represented, must be enumerated the following :—

That gluttony and lasciviousness were their principal crimes.

That avarice was common among them.

That there was no honouring God in spirit and in truth.

That they were ambitious, persecuting and abominably superstitious.

That they were great instruments of sedition.

That their giving *veniæ*—pardon for the omission of duties—and calling upon the Hierarchies of Heaven were hypocritical absurdities.

That their upholding sanctuary was a wilful conniving at the greatest crimes.

That they were great cheats and imposters, exposing among their most famed reliquaries such things as the Holy Shroud, which had enwrapped our Saviour's body after it was taken from the Cross, the hair of the Holy Virgin, holy roods, which wept, or spoke, or bled, miraculous oils, or water, or herbs, which were asserted to cure all ailments.

That they ordered masses to be sung for the

dead, in order that they might enrich themselves with the fees.

That they asserted that from the graves of their principal saints miraculous oils and perfumes arose.

That Jesus Christ himself taught St Catharine of Sienna to read.

That all their conduct was ordered by expediency, a common saying among them being, '*Frustra fit per plura, quod fieri potest per panciora*,' or, it is folly to go about when there lies a short cut before us.

That they established confraternities, who professed to pray for and achieve the relief of souls in purgatory, but who were little better than swindlers.

That their doctrines of purgatory were more established for the profit of the living than for the comfort of the dead.

That they were idolators of mammon.

That their highest officials were effeminate and wanton.

That they were ever uttering vicious and faulty arguments.

And that they were altogether blinded by

superstition, or by their own interests and
passions, making together a formidable in-
dictment.

The cynical and querulous Barclay, in his
'Ship of Fooles,' p. 119, thus paints these
monks :—

> ' The Abbot and Prior, and also their Convent
> Are so blinded with unhappy covetise,
> That with their own can they not be content,
> But to have more they always meanes devise
> Yea, in so much that some have found a gyse
> To fayne their brethren taken in captivitie,
> That they may begge so by authoritie,
> They fayne miracles, where non were ever done—
> And all for lucre ; some other range about
> To gather and begge with some fayned pardon,
> And at the ale-house at night all drinketh out.
> So run these beggars in company rowte,
> By streetes, tavernes, towns, and villages,
> No place can well be free of their outrages.
> Some begge for buildings, some for reliques newe
> Of holy Saintes, of countries farre and strange ;
> And with their wordes fayned and untrue,
> For cause of lucre about they runne and range :
> But in a simple village, farme or grange,
> Whereat these beggars most simplemen may finde,
> With their false bones as relickes, they them blinde.'

According to the famous Black Book of the
Monasteries, which was prepared by commis-

sioners appointed to visit and enquire into the
state of the religious houses, and which was in the
year 1536 laid upon the table of the House of
Commons, it is quoted from an authority,* that
a large proportion of the monks resident in
England were living in habits of dissoluteness.
It also declared the monastic system to be in
ruins. It was upon that book or series of
reports that the first Act of Dissolution, 27 Hen.
VIII, cap. 28, was passed. Among the many
reports to be found in this 'Book' is one by
John Hales, private secretary to Sir Thomas
Cromwell, containing the following passage :—
' According to your pleasure and commandment,
the Papistical denne of idle and utterly unlearned
beasts at Soulbie is broken up and dispersed, and
your servant is in possession.' There is another
from one Dr Richard Layton to the same personage, to this purport:—'At Lewis, I found corruption of both kinds—*et quod pejus est traturas.*
The Superior hath confessed to me treason in his
preaching. . . . At Battle, I found the Abbot
and all his convent, saveing one or two, great
day-lay sinners and traiturs. The Abbot is the

* Strype's Memorials.

varaste hayve bette and buserde, and the arrants
chorle that ever I see in all other places whereas I come, especially the black sort of devilish
monks. Surely I think they be past amend-
ment, and that God hath utterly withdrawn His
grace from them.' *

A modern author asserts—' By the acquisition
and in some respects the enjoyment, or at least,
ostentation of great riches, the ancient monastic
orders had forfeited much of the public esteem.'†
And again—'That their extreme licentiousness
was sometimes hardly concealed by the cowl of
sanctity.' And once again—'That in the very
best view, however, that can be taken of
monasteries their existence is deeply injurious to
the general morals of a nation.' And finally—
'Their frauds, however, were less atrocious than
the savage bigotry with which they maintained
their own system and infected the laity.'

But for all these sweeping charges, there were
undoubtedly many monasteries and many more
monks, to which and to whom they did in no
way apply. Time, however, has flown by, the

---

* Brit. Mus. Ags. Ca., No. 4160, Art. 13.
† Hallam's Middle Ages, vol. ii., p. 5.

G

victims of the system have all been long, long since swept away, death, ruin, and insolvency have rolled over them and they are gone down to the bottom of the social scale, out of sight and out of hearing. The day of mourning has even long since passed, and in England 'the monks of old' are looked back upon as a lost species of whom fossil bones reappear from time to time, exciting curiosity and withal a share of undeserved repugnance. Despoiled and proscribed they no longer hold a place in history among the living, though their ancient spirit, their antique grandeur, the high position they once held in the destinies of the world and their indomitable labours in the cause of Christianity and civilization, rear for them throughout Christendom, and will throughout all time, an indestructible, ineffaceable monument.

The great body of men, however, who during so many early ages, peopled the monasteries and recruited the permanent army of prayer and charity, rendered to science, to literature and agriculture, services, the benefits of which we, in our days, still reap. The constant prosperity of conventual lands, the excellence of the methods

of culture, and the good rendered to the peasants
by these industrious, persevering and always
resident proprietors, who consecrated the greater
portion of their revenues to the culture and
improvement of their patrimony, testify the
early—and therefore, as examples, the lasting—
benefits bestowed upon agriculture. The many
literary and scientific embers of monastic eru-
dition, congregated as time-eternal specimens
in many foreign and home museums, should
effectually typify to the minds of modern scep-
tics, that to the monk we owe most of the
unmatched blessings of literary and scientific
life.

The monasteries of old were the great school-
houses of study and knowledge, their cowled
and robed occupiers, the bearers of the illuminating torch. Within these despised and
desecrated walls too, did heavenly charity reign
absolute sovereign. 'Weep with the unhappy,'
instructed St Columba. It was a precept
always borne in mind. It was not merely in
giving alms and bestowing a practical generosity
and hospitality that they were alone famed, but
it was equally for their benign and paternal

sympathy, their active and cordial interest in the people, that still causes their name to be revered in those parts of the world where gratitude and regret are not unknown qualities. What nobly said St Bernard—the man who shed such unmatched glory over the frock and tonsure of the monk—'The friendship of the poor constitutes us the friends of kings, but the love of poverty makes kings of us.' Was it not among the cloisters of the monk that the Christian rebels against the abuses of power sought and found a ready haven? There the victims of tyranny, injustice and might, found a sure and safe asylum. There too, was a sepulchre, not only for kings, nobles and the great ones of earth, but one also for the feeble, the lowly and the poor. There slept in peace, in the midst of perpetual prayer, the exile, the outlaw and the criminal. From the very dawn, and throughout the duration of the Christian ages, the cloister was the universal and mighty nursery of great souls, while its most brilliant and enduring glory was the vigorous temper it gave to Christians, the fertile and generous discipline which it imposed upon thousands of heroic spirits. These services and these triumphs, immeasurable and eternal as they were, attain their just recognition from a benefited posterity, only under the survey of history.

Where now are all these much abused, yet much to be commended, institutions? What has betided the magnificent structures, which in so many different parts of the metropolis upreared their lofty towers and carved minarets to the sky? Where flows now that fountain of pure and inoffensive happiness once swelling so abundantly within their consecrated walls? Whither pours now that generous stream of perfect charity and sympathy and goodwill which had flowed through ages in waves of incessant and fruitful fluctuation? Where are the fair and noble churches which so many generations of our forefathers frequented to seek consolation, courage and strength to enable them to contend against the evils of life? Where, oh where, are those cloisters that offered ever a safe and noble asylum to all, where every science was promoted, every art perfected, where the hungry were always satisfied, the naked clothed, the miserable comforted, the ignorant instructed? Where are they all gone? They are evermore ruined, exhausted, dried up, dismantled and destroyed. A mighty interdict was suddenly cast upon their world of beauty, piety, generosity and usefulness. Their Carthusian world of peaceful sanctity, of king protecting intercession, of penitence and benediction, of industry and philanthropy, was signed away—swept from the broad surface of the metropolitan area, through an insatiable cupidity, by tyrants, sophists and rhetoricians, for their own glory and aggrandisement. Forth went the cruel and mischievous mandate, and the hand of the destroyer smote one and all, both great and small. Few are the ruins left in the present century to attest the glories that have been, and those few stained by a thousand ignoble profanations, subsist merely as monuments of ruin and folly. The inoffensive dwellers amid the numerous cenobitical homes, were scattered as chaff before the wind, some condemned to apostacy, others to martyrdom, but the greater part to expatriation, while cattle ruminated in their roofless vestibules and ruined cloisters, and eat grass beside their overthrown altars. Denounced for their disorders, abuses and scandals, uncredited with the inappreciable benefits they had through centuries bestowed on mankind, 'the monks of old,' were in England, amid the moral volcano that of a sudden ravaged the Christian world, placed under the ban of humanity, seized in their cells, expelled from their lawful dwelling-places, robbed of their patrimony, and cast forth as vagabonds and outlaws, without asylum, and without resource upon the world.

But even though it was necessary in Protestant England to confiscate and suppress the monasteries, why should the exquisitely wrought buildings have been overthrown, and not one stone left standing on another? Westminster and St Albans tell us what they were. The ruins might at least have been preserved, and future generations been permitted to behold their funereal beauty—the remains of a one time inimitable art and sublime architecture. Vandalism only paused when there was nothing left to overthrow and crumble down.

Part Third

Digest of the London Religious Houses

SECTION I

OUR space will not admit of our doing more than refer most cursorily to the majority of the many religious establishments within and around ancient London during the zenith of their prosperity, in the early part of the sixteenth century, and just before the axe of the grasping and unscrupulous king was laid to the root of the memorable tree of monachism.

The number of these erections—wherein dwelt the Palidins of moral and intellectual manhood, 'the monks of old,' termed as they have indifferently been, *Milites Christi, Chevaliers de l'Eglise*, and *Chevalerie de Dieu*,—amounted to nearly fifty of the first class, the second or lower class being much more numerous; but with the latter we do not, in this work, purpose to deal.

In the succeeding epitome we shall divide the various monastic corporations or institutions into different classes or divisions, adopting the titles of the several denominations by which they were known, viz. :—Abbeys or Convents, Priories, Friaries, Nunneries, Colleges, Hospitals, and Fraternities or Guilds.

SECTION II

THE ABBEYS OR CONVENTS

1. WESTMINSTER.—Immemorially known, this great ecclesiastical structure, established on the grandest scale was the most ancient the wealthiest, the most powerful, the most extensive and

most frequented of all those wondrous and numerous cenobitical institutions which made England the very Paradise of monachism. Of the foundation of this stately structure we have many varied and some absurd accounts. By one it has been attempted to be palmed on no less illustrious a personage than St Peter, to whom it was dedicated. This pious fraud was attempted by Abbot Wulfine in the reign of Edward the Confessor. Another account refers it to the imaginary reign of King Lucias. In the uncertainty that prevails on the subject, we cannot do better than adopt the solution given by most of the old historical commentators and attribute the foundation to Sebert, King of the Saxons, about the year 610. It was reared, quoths legend, on the ruins of a temple dedicated by the heathen Saxons to Apollo, that was thrown down by an earthquake. The spot on which this sumptuous structure was built, was a waste of land known as Thornie Island, from its being over-run with thorns and briars, and from its insulation by a curving branch of the Thames, known as Long Ditch. · Like many another of its sacred order, it was destroyed by

the pagan Danes, and subsequently rebuilt in
the year 958, by King Edgar, who by charter in
969, richly endowed it, granting it many exceptional privileges. A few years later it was
again subjected to the ruthless ravages of the
Danes, but was afterwards restored with more
than its original splendour, by Edward the
Confessor, during the period intervening between
1049 and 1066. It was consecrated by that
King with great pomp and solemnity, and by
his charters confirmed in all its ancient rights
and privileges. He likewise endowed it with
additional manors and granted it still greater
immunities. In addition, he assigned to it,
by special charter, the great privilege of
Sanctuary.

William the Conqueror was crowned in the
Abbey, and thus set an example which has been
ever since followed by all subsequent kings and
queens. William was a great benefactor to this
Abbey, granting it, during his reign, no less
than sixteen charters. Henry the Third erected
a chapel at the east end and dedicated it to the
Virgin Mary, the first stone of which was laid
in the year 1221. The principal building

having, during this reign, shown manifest signs
of decay, Henry caused the greater portion of it
to be taken down, and after great expense and
labour he carried on the rebuilding during a
period of twenty-seven years. He did not live
to complete the magnificent design he had in
contemplation. Indeed, it is generally asserted
that it was not fully finished, even to its present
incomplete state, until the reign of Henry VII,
who in the year 1502 caused the Chapel of the
Virgin Mary and a tower adjoining to be pulled
down, and on the site thereof he erected the
present stately and magnificent edifice denominated Henry VII Chapel.

The two western towers were not fully completed until after the Reformation, while the
great central tower, a part of the original grand
design, remains, to the shame of the metropolis,
unreared at the present day. Henry the Third, to
whom as we have shown we are so much
indebted for this peerless jewel amid our public
edifices, in the year 1257, granted by Charter to
the Abbot and convent of Westminster the right
of holding a weekly market or fair. Edward
the First, as a memento of his having reduced

Scotland, brought from there in the year 1296, the famous block of marble whereon from time immemorial the Scottish Kings had been crowned, and on which was engraven this distich—

'Ni fallat fatum, Scoti hunc quocumque locatum,
Inveniunt lapidem, reguare tenenter ibidem.'

Edward caused this stone to be fixed beneath a large wooden chair, which has been ever since used as the Coronation Seat for our kings and queens.

In the year 1352 Westminster was, by Act of Parliament, constituted one of the then ten towns of England where markets for the sale of staple commodities were to be perpetually held. The territories of this lordly abbey extended far beyond the limits known by its name. They compassed on one side alone the whole distance between Chelsea and Whitehall, then known as York House. While to the west they reached as far as Kensington, including the parishes now known as St George's, St James', St Paul's and St Anne's, and the entire district of St Martin's-in-the-fields. In addition to these large territories were the outlying manors of

Hendon, Hampstead and Paddington, while the Kilburn and Clerkenwell Nunneries belonged to the foundation of this abbey. The revenues, on its surrender on the 16th January 1539, amounted to £3977, 6s 4d, an income equal at the present day to £30,000, so changed is the price of land and value of gold.

The abbey narrowly escaped destruction when in the fulness of his power, the Protector, Somerset, ruled over the land. It is a well authenticated fact that it was his design to have pulled it down in order to supply the necessary stone material for the building of the palace he began to erect in the Strand, and which has been ever since known as Somerset House. He was only diverted from his impious intent by the large bribe of not fewer than fourteen manors. From 1377 to 1547, the Commons of England held most of their Parliaments in the Super-Chapter House of the Abbey. While Henry II breathed his last in the Jerusalem Chamber, which then formed part of the Abbot's Lodgings. No space or description could sufficiently do justice to the sumptuous glories of this magnificent ecclesiastical structure. Many abler pens have been engaged upon the attempt, and to their productions we must refer our readers for fuller and better particulars.

2. St Saviours.—This abbey situate near St John's Court in Bermondsey, was founded in the year 1082, by Alwin Child, a citizen of London, for an order known as *Cluniacs*. The foundation with all the benefactions pertaining thereto, was subsequently confirmed by the charter of William Rufus, who likewise conferred upon the Prior and monks, the Manor of Bermondsey, and at his own cost, erected a beautiful and spacious conventual church, for the use and accommodation of the monks. This, however, being at first a priory, and an offshoot of one in France, was amongst other foreign foundations in England, sequestered by Edward the Third, in the year 1371, who appointed Richard Denton, an Englishman, Prior thereof. In consideration whereof, and of the sum of two hundred marks, Richard II demised the same in the year 1380. This Priory, in the year 1399, was converted into an Abbey, when Pope Boniface named John Attelborough the first Abbot thereof. This house was surrendered in

the year 1539, and shortly after destroyed by
Sir Thomas John Pope, to whom it was granted.

Attached to this Abbey was a dock, called
'Savory's, Dock,' and a valuable mill. Its
annual revenues were £474, 14s 4d.

3. THE CHARTREUSE was founded in Smithfield, for Carthusians, in the year 1371, by Sir
Walter Manny, in honour of God and the Virgin
Mary, as we are told, and by the appellation of
'The Salutation of the Mother of God.' The
title of Charter House is a corruption of the
French appellative *Chartreuse*, that being the
designation of the place where the first
Carthusian monk founded his order in France,
for which reason, all Carthusian convents were
styled *Chartreuse*. Sir Walter Manny, who was
a most successful commander during the French
wars, under the third Edward, first intended to
found a college, for a warden, dean, and twelve
secular priests, but changing his intention, he in
conjunction with Northburgh, Bishop of London,
founded a Priory, for twenty-four monks of the
above rigid order. The London Charter House
monks bore a high reputation for sanctity, and
from all we can glean, deserved it. Froude says

it was the best ordered house in England. The
last Prior but one, John Houghton, subscribed to
the King's supremacy in 1534, but was soon
after tried, convicted, and executed for his
opposition to the royal will. Three years after,
William Trafford, the last Prior, subscribed to
the royal supremacy. It was suppressed in
1538, when its revenue amounted to £642, 0s 4d.
It was thereupon conferred upon Sir Thomas
Audley, Speaker of the House of Commons.
By royal letter patent of 22nd June, 1611,
subsequently confirmed in 1628, by Act of
Parliament, a hospital for pensioners and
scholars was founded by Thomas Sutton, citizen
and girdler of London, by whom it had been
purchased and fitted up, at a cost of £20,000.
In addition to which munificent outlay, Sutton
endowed this foundation with fifteen manors,
and other lands, yielding yearly the sum of
£4493, 19s 10d.

4. EASTMINSTER. — Otherwise denominated
New Abbey, Grace Abbey or the Abbey of the
Graces, was founded in East Smithfield by King
Edward the Third, in 1359, for Cistercians. It
was situated to the north-east of the Tower, and

without the walls, and was possessed by several charters of the manors of Gravesend, of Poplar, and of several others in Kent, also of rents in Woolwich. It had a special charter from Edward the Third. By patent of Henry the Fourth, it became further enriched by divers manors in the counties of Somerset, Devon and Cornwall. This house was made subject to that of Beaulieu, whose abbot first presided over its destinies. A fair was granted to be held here by Henry the Third, from the ' Eve of Pentecost, till the octaves of the Trinity.' At the general suppression, its annual income was returned at £546, 10s. It was surrendered in the year 1539. In a short space the monastery was utterly razed and, with the ground attached, converted into a market.

SECTION III

THE PRIORIES

1. ELSING PRIORY was situated in Monk-well Street, close beside the church of St Elphege

or St Alphage, which indeed is a remnant of the Priory. It became subsequent to the dissolution the site of Sion College. It was founded in the year 1329, by William Elsing, citizen and mercer, and was dedicated by him to St Mary—originally for a college of seculars. But in the year 1340, he refounded it as a Priory for a Prior and five regular Canons of the order of St Augustine, this number being subsequently increased. A part of the Conventual Church was, after its surrender in 1539, made part of the present parish church, the porch whereof, with its sculptured heads and pointed arches, still vouch for its antiquity. Its revenues amounted to £193, 15s 5d, according to Dugdale, and to £239, 13s 11d, according to Speed.

2. THE HOLY TRINITY.—This Priory, otherwise known as that of Christ Church and of St Michael's, and which was designated in its original Charter as the '*Prioratus de Chrichurch*,' was situated near Aldgate, just within the walls on the right hand and was founded by Matilda, daughter of Malcolm, King of Scotland, and Queen to Henry I of England, generally known as Queen Maud, in the year 1109, for

regular Canons of the order of St Augustine.
Norman was the first Prior and is asserted to
have been the first canon regular of his order
in England. The Queen, by special charter,
endowed this Priory with a yearly stipend of
£25 and with the proceeds of the port of
Aldgate, the receipts from whence were no
doubt considerable. She also gave the Prior
and convent the churches of Brackyng, St
Augustine Passy, St Edmund's and All Hallows-
on-the-wall. Several subsequent charters were
granted to it by King Stephen, Henry the
Second and others increasing its buildings, its
income and its privileges. The church was
large, magnificently decorated and possessed a
peal of nine bells. This Priory was rich in
lands and rentals, and became one of the
wealthiest monastic institutions in London, and
surpassing many older in foundation, while being
of greater pretension as regarded its extent of
buildings. Its Prior was always elected Alder-
man for Portsoken ward. The Priors were very
hospitable and feasted both rich and poor
sumptuously. It was the first of the religious
houses upon which the grasping Henry set his

fangs and was the first dissolved. It was surrendered on the 4th February 1531 and by the King assigned to Sir Thomas Audley, the Speaker of the House of Commons, afterwards Lord Chancellor, who like other Vandals of that age, razed to the ground the handsome church with all its fine sepulchral monuments—among which were those of Baldwin and Matilda, the children of King Stephen—and the whole of the conventual buildings. This Priory received the special countenance of the Pope, being commended by His Holiness in a charter of the Cardinal of St Martin, Legate of the Apostolic See. The Pope, too, by a Bull,* absolved the Prior from all jurisdiction, even from that of the King.

3. ST BARTHOLOMEW.—This was a Priory of Black Canons founded by one Rahere, 'a man sprung from low kynage,' in the reign of Henry the Second, and about the year 1102. The founder was minstrel to Henry the First, and as Stow says, ' was a pleasant witted gentleman,' but wearying of that vocation, he founded this celebrated house and became the first Prior of

* Stow

his own foundation. It was erected on the present site of St Bartholomew's Hospital—which still embraces many interesting parts of the ancient Priory—on a 'right unclean site, a marsh, dunge and feuny with water ever abounding.' Henry the Second granted to the Prior and his Canons the privilege of holding for three days, viz: 'the eve, the next day and the morrow,' of Bartholomew-tide, an annual fair within their own precincts, in a part known as Bartholomew Close, and which privilege was the origin of the yearly orgy, known for so many years as Bartholomew Fair. The famous Court of Pie-Powder was held during the continuance of this jubilee. This monastery, with its extensive precincts was enclosed on all sides by a strong wall,* wherein besides all the numerous monastic offices, was a large garden, a spacious court, an extensive cemetery, the mulberry garden and the famed close. The same founder, Rahere, originated the well known hospital of the same name, on a plot of land adjoining the convent walls, placing the government thereof in the hands of the authorities of the Priory. In

* *Londini Illustrata.*

1410 the Priory was rebuilt, considerably enlarged and became a magnificent structure. It
was surrendered in 1539, when its revenues
amounted to the sum of £653, 15s.

4. St Mary Overie—So called from being
dedicated to one, Mary, its reputed founder—
the daughter of the ferryman, whose pence were
put by for the foundation and erection—and
from lying over the water in Southwark. It
was refounded for Canons Regular of St Augustine, by William Pont del 'Arche and William
Dauncey, Norman Knights, in the year 1106.
Some authorities assert this to have been the
first religious house in London, and to have been
founded before the conquest by the beforenamed
Mary, a virgin, for Nuns and Sisters. This
house of Sisters was afterwards, by Swithin, a
noble lady, converted into a College of Priests.*
The ferry was anciently the *trajectus* of the
Roman Military Way, denominated Watling
Street, which ran on the west side of old
Winchester House. This Priory was destroyed
by fire about the year 1207. A temporary
building was thereupon erected and used until

* Stripe's Stow, vol. ii, p. 773.

in the year 1215, Peter de Rupibus, otherwise
Peter de Roches, Bishop of Winchester, removed
it to another site near at hand, called the Armery,
and then rebuilt it with a large church and
considerable splendour. He dedicated it to St
Mary Magdalen and refounded the Priory for
Canons Regular by endowing it with the annual
sum of £344. The Convent afterwards became
poor, so much so that the Prior and Canons
uttered a somewhat memorable public reproach,*
which had a beneficial result. The monastic
buildings, during this period of poverty, becom-
ing sadly impaired, were wholly and nobly
restored by the poet Gower towards the close of
the fourteenth century. He was married and
buried within the Priory Church. His monument, still enshrined, is worthy a visit. The
first Prior was Aldgod, the last Bartholomew
Luisted. It was surrendered in October 1540,
when its revenues amounted to £654 6s 6d.
The church was purchased from King Henry
VIII by the parishioners, with the assistance of
the Bishop of Winchester, and thereafter became
the parish church, under the title of St Saviour's,

* Taylor's Annals.

Southwark.   It would appear that some portion
of the conventual buildings, in the reign of
James I, were fashioned into and endowed for a
parish school, while other parts, including the
'Lady Chapel,' are interwoven into the present
parish church, forming a rare ecclesiastical
antiquity.

5. St Mary of Bethelem.—Without Bishop's
Gate, on the east side of the mere or moor called
Moorfields and in the parish of St Botolph, was
the famous Hospital of Bethelem or House of
Bethlem-on-the-Moor, vulgarly termed Bedlam.
It was originally founded as a Priory of Canons
for brethren and sisters, by Simon Fitz-Mary,
one of the Sheriffs of London in the year 1246.
The founder richly endowed this monastic home
with all his lands in the parish of St Botolph by
a certain deed of gift still extant.   King
Edward the Third, in the fourteenth year of his
reign, granted a protection within the city for
the brethren under the title of '*Militiæ beatæ
Mariæ de Bethlem.*'   It was surrendered about
the year 1546 when Henry the Eighth gave the
buildings to the city, the mayor and commonalty
having previously purchased the patronage of it,

and it was at once opened as a hospital for distracted people. Subsequently this foundation was, on account of its bad situation, limited accommodation and ruinous condition, removed to a large structure in Moorfields, a portion of the present handsome building, the foundation whereof was commenced in the year 1675.

6. THE PRIORY OF ST JOHN.—This foundation was only a branch of the famed and powerful body, which at one time swayed the destinies of the world—the Knights Hospitallers of the order of St John of Jerusalem, and who were known also as the Knights of Rhodes and Knights of Malta. The founder of this house— situate near the Nunnery at Clerkenwell—was Jordan Brisset, the wealthy baron who had previously founded and ·endowed that nunnery. It would appear he purchased from the prioress and nuns of that establishment, ten acres of land in exchange for twenty acres of his Manor of Willinghale in Kent, whereon he erected a noble Monastery, during the year 1110. The magnificent church which was not completed for several years after, contained some side chapels of most elaborate workmanship and ornamenta-

tion, with a tower that was renowned throughout England for its exquisite symmetry and carving, as well as for its being richly wrought in gilt and enamel. The conventual buildings covered a large space of ground, and were enclosed by a stout lofty wall, with a magnificent gateway, surmounted with side turrets and a species of keep—still standing. The buildings were consecrated by Heraclius, Patriarch of Jerusalem. Originally founded in 1048, they were for a long period, a very poor order and much despised, but of a sudden, through their warlike habits and heroic deeds, and by divers numerous gifts and wealthy endowments, they rose to be one of the wealthiest communities in Christendom. They became a regular monastic corporation in 1099, and a military order in 1118. They were in process of time, both at home and abroad, invested by different monarchs with many extraordinary privileges. At one time their order possessed no less than 19,000 manors, in different parts of Christendom, while it comprised more than double that number of brethren. The first Prior or Grand Master of the Clerkenwell Priory was Garnerius de Neapoli, and the last Sir William Weston. To such a high standard of power, honour and wealth, did this mighty order attain in England, that the Grand Master ranked as the first baron in the kingdom, and ~~who~~, in state and grandeur, well-nigh equalled royalty itself. He possessed supreme authority over all the preceptories, bailiwicks or commanderies throughout Great Britain. To such a pitch of popularity did they at one time attain, that in 1312, on the dissolution of the order of the 'Knights Templars,' who followed the rule of St Augustine, the whole possessions of the latter were, in the year 1323, bestowed on them, a result which offered no slight increase to their already great wealthy and high degree. The ordinary dress of this order was a black mantle, with a white cross of eight spikes on the left breast. The Superiors were distinguished by wearing white robes, with red crosses and facings. Beneath this seemingly peaceful-looking robe, they harnessed their bodies with entire suits of mail. The patroness of the Knights of St John was, 'the sweet Mother of God.' This large house was suppressed by

Henry the Eighth on Ascension Day, in the year 1540, when according to Dugdale, its revenues were valued at the yearly sum of £2385, 12s 8d, and according to Strype, at £3385, 19s 8d. In 1550 the church and buildings of this monastery came into the hands of the ambitious Vandal, Edward Seymour, Duke of Somerset, the Protector of the Kingdom, who ruthlessly caused the whole — except the still existing gateway—to be demolished, and the materials thereof, to be used in the erection of his stately palace of Somerset House.

———

SECTION IV

THE FRIARIES

1. BLACK FRIARS.—In Knight's London, the following concise description is given of this great monastery : ' Yet here '—the precincts of Blackfriars—' three centuries ago stood the

great religious house of the Dominican or Black
Friars, who were the lords of the precinct, shut-
ting out all civic authority, and enclosing within
their four gates a busy community of shop-
keepers and artificers. Here in the hallowed
dust of the ancient church were the royal and
the noble buried, and their gilded tombs proclaimed their virtues to posterity. Here parliaments have sat, and pulled down odious
favourites. Here kings have required exorbi-
tant aids from complaining subjects. Here
Wolsey pronounced the sentence of divorce on
the persecuted Catharine.' The following is a copy
of the Charter granted by Edward the Second
to the Black Friars. 'To all, etc. . . . Whereas
Gregory de Rochefly, our Mayor of London,
and the other Barons of the said city, at our
instance, have commonly and unanimously
granted to the Venerable Father Robert, Archbishop of Canterbury and his assigns, two Lanes
contiguous to his place of Castle Baynard and
the Tower of Mountfichet, to be stopped up for
the enlargement of the aforesaid place and to
enclose them. And We, understanding from the
aforesaid Mayor and Barons of the said city,

that the said Archbishop hath already prepared
a better way and more convenient for the said
Commonalty than the foresaid Lanes were, We,
to the said Archbishop and his assigns for us
and our heirs as much as in us is, do grant,
ratify and confirm the foresaid Grant, so that
our said Barons of London by occasion of their
foresaid Grant, nor the Archbishop nor his
assigns, on account of the said changing of the
ways, be accused or molested for time to come
before our justices itinerants, at the Tower of
London upon cause of Purpresenture made of the
foresaid Lanes.   In testimony whereof, etc.'
This monastery was 'of the fee of St Johnne
and thereby greatlie privileged.' It was a vast
and wealthy house.   After receiving many
special grants and immunities it was in Henry
VI's reign incorporated by Act of Parliament,
'Whereby they'—the friars—'might prescribe
and did always use and keep the liberty invio-
lately and clearly exempted from the citizens.'
An authority informs us that 'In Queen Elizabeth's time this Black Friars was much inhabited
by noblemen and gentlemen as before.   For the
spaciousness of it, Parliaments, notably "the

Black Parliament," often sat there and noble personages were there harboured.'* This monastery survived for many years the general dissolution. The citizens of London were for a long time jealous of the privileges of so large a space and so numerous a body politic within their own walls, and many a fruitless action on behalf of the civic authorities was taken against the special immunities enjoyed by the Black Friars in the reign of Mary and Elizabeth.

2. GREY FRIARS was situated in Ludgate Street, near the present site of Christ's Hospital, in the parish of St Nicholas Shambles. This monastery was founded by one John Ewin, mercer, in 1225 for Franciscans. Queen Margaret, consort to Edward First, in the year 1306, commenced the erection of a very spacious and handsome church which took twenty-one years to complete. Sir Richard Whittington in 1421, added at his own expense a large library for the use of the monks, and laid out £400 in furnishing the same. It was surrendered in 1588. The church became subsequently a parish one, but was utterly destroyed by the great fire

* Maitland, vol. ii. p. 951.

in 1666. There is an evident error in the amount of income assigned to it by Dugdale. These mendicants of the order of St Francis of Assisi seem to have possessed great power of persuasion, for they raised vast sums for their buildings from among the rich. Four queens were herein interred, viz., Margaret, second queen of Edward the First, Isabella, queen of Edward the Second, Joan queen of Edward Bruce, King of Scotland, and Isabella the titular Queen of the Isle of Man. In addition it formed the last resting-place of many other royal and noble personages.

3. CRUTCHED FRIARS.—It was more properly designated Crouched or Crossed Friars, or the House of the Friars of the Holy Cross. The order was instituted, or at least reformed, about the year 1169, by Gerard, Prior of St Mary de Morello at Bologna. They came to England in 1244, and after their arrival in London they demanded from the opulent a house to live in, declaring that they were privileged by the Pope, and were exempt from all reproach, and that he had delegated to them power to excommunicate those who were hardly

enough to reprove them. Such an assertion
was quite enough in those credulous days, and
consequently two citizens, Ralph Hosier and
William Sabernes were wise enough to accom-
modate these friars with a house in Hart Street,
Tower Street, near the walls on the west side of
Goodman's fields and themselves became friars
of it. This was in the year 1298. Several
grants by other citizens led to a considerable
extension of the original buildings. Robert
Adams was the first Prior and Edmund
Streatam the last. The friars originally carried
in their hands an iron cross, which they afterwards, as their means increased, changed into
one of silver. They also wore a cross made of
red cloth on the back of their robes. It was
surrendered in 1536, when its revenue amounted
to £52, 13s 4d. Two Dutch fraternities subsequently settled here, but at the present day not
a vestige of the Friary remains.

4. AUSTIN FRIARS. — The convent of the
Augustine Friars, or to give them their proper
designation of the Friars Eremites of the order
of St Augustine, was founded by Humfrey
Bohun, Earl of Hereford and Essex, in the year

1253. It was considerably enlarged in 1344
A large number of persons of high rank were
interred within the church, in consequence of
the peculiar sanctity with which it is asserted
these friars filled the earth. The monuments
were many of them co-equal in beauty to the
ancient ones of Westminster, and cost thousands.
In its chapter-house were interred many of the
Barons who fell on the 14th April 1471, on the
Heath of Gladsmoor, near Barnet, where fell too,
the last of the Barons. This conventual establishment was surrendered on the 12th November
1538 at which time its revenues amounted to
£57. The church stood as one of the greatest
curiosities of modern London until the lament-
able fire of a few years back.

5. WHITE FRIARS.—This order—the Friars of
Our Lady of Mount Carmel—was founded in
London, in 1241, by Sir Richard Grey, ancestor
of the Lords Grey of Codnor. The correct title of
the fraternity, was ' *Fratres B. Mariae de Monte
Carmelo.*' The order had its origin in Mount
Carmel in Syria, where, said they, dwelt Elias and
Eliseus the prophets. There, in process of time,
many Anchorites settled, who afterwards by

means of Almeric, Bishop of Antioch, the Pope's
Legate, were assembled together under one
ecclesiastical government. Upon the same spot,
were laid the foundations of a convent. There
Almeric reared up a monastery for them, in lieu
of the dens and caves they had theretofore
existed in. The order was first introduced into
Europe, about the year 1216, by Albert,
Patriarch of Jerusalem, and legate to Pope
Innocent III. These hermits of Mount Carmel,
like the Dominicans and Minorites, at first
professed begging in Europe. Then they were
permitted to preach and receive confessions.
Their order was confirmed by Popes
Honorius III, Gregory IX, Innocent IV and
others. Their robe was white with a black
hood. Ralph Freshburne, a Carmelite Friar,
laid the first foundation of the order in England
in 1224, near Alnwick, in Northumberland, at
which time, it would appear, they did not
observe celibacy, nor did they shave or annoint
themselves. King Edward I, after their induction into London, gave to the Prior and brethren
of the order, a plot of ground in Fleet Street,
between the Temple and Salisbury Court,

whereupon to build a house. This was afterwards refounded and enlarged by Hugh Courtenay, Earl of Devonshire, in the year 1350, and in 1407, the church was sumptuously rebuilt by the celebrated Knight, Sir Robert Knolles. Attached to this Monastery, among its other immunities and liberties, was that of Sanctuary. The district so privileged, was then called, and long after known, as ' Alsatia.' This house was surrendered in 1539, when its annual income as returned by Dugdale was £26, 7s 3d, and by another authority as £63, 2s 4d. The Sanctuary was abolished by Act of Parliament in 1697.

SECTION V

NUNNERIES

1. St John the Baptist was founded by Richard I in the year 1189, and refounded by

Sir Thomas Lovel in 1570, for Benedictines. It was situated near a spot known as Holywell, in the then rustic village of Soredich, modernized into Shoreditch. The refounder endowed the Prioress and nuns of this convent with considerable property. He was buried there, in the chapel of his own erection, and, as his monument, his grateful beneficiaries engraved on each window of the chapel the couplet:

> ' All the nunnes in Holywell
> Pray for the soul of Sir Thomas Lovell.'

This convent was surrendered in the year 1539 when, according to Speed, its revenues amounted to £347 1s 3d.

2. ST HELEN'S.—This nunnery was situated in Bishopsgate Street and gives its title to the present large square or court of that name. The site of Crosby Square also formed part of the original estate belonging to this house, until a Prioress, named Alicia Ashfield, sold it in the year 1466 to Sir John Crosby. This convent was founded by one, William Basing, a goldsmith, asserted by Stow to have been Dean of St Paul's in the year 1212, for Benedictines. It

was suppressed in 1539. The church pertaining
to the convent was afterwards created the
parish church of Great St Helen's. The dedica-
tion was originally to St Helen, mother of
Constantine the Great, and afterwards to the
Holy Cross, though the first title seems to have
been familiarly retained. Its revenues, according to Dugdale, amounted to £314 2s 6d. A
large portion of the original structure, with the
crypt, forms part of the present ancient and
picturesque church which is well worth a visit.

3. THE MINORIES otherwise designated the
Abbey of St Clare, or the Abbey of the
Minoresses of St Mary of the order of St Clare.
It was founded in 1293 by Edmund, Earl of
Lancaster, Leicester and Darby, brother to King
Edward the First, at the instigation of his wife,
Blanche, Queen of Navarre, who brought over
the minoresses with her and established them in
the building prepared for their reception. They
soon became popular among the citizens of
London, who enriched the nunnery by divers
grants of land and houses. An extensive and
very remunerative farm was attached to this
convent. The Abbess and nuns also enjoyed

many extensive liberties granted to them by
several special charters in the reigns of
Edward II, Henry IV, Henry V, Henry VI and
Edward IV. They professed to serve God, the
Blessed Virgin, and St Francis. The last Abbess
was Dame Elizabeth Savage, who surrendered
this convent to Henry VIII in 1539, when its
revenues were estimated at £418, 8s 5d.

4. CLERKENWELL.—This was founded in the
year 1100 for Benedictines or black nuns, by
Jordan Brisset, a wealthy Baron—the same who
founded the Priory of St John of Jerusalem.
He gave to his chaplain, Robert, fourteen acres
adjoining Clerkenwell, a beautiful rural village,
whereon to erect a convent, which was no
sooner erected and dedicated to the honour of
God and the Assumption of the Virgin Mary,
than he placed therein a certain number of nuns
and appointed a Prioress. Benefactions of lands,
tenements and specie poured in upon these nuns,
who were among the most popular in the
metropolis. The hall and ambulatory of this
convent were exquisite specimens of art and
architecture. Within the former were frequently performed, before a select audience,

mysteries or sacred dramatic plays. The first Prioress was Dame Christina, the last Isabella Sackville of the family of the Duke of Dorset. Its revenues at its suppression in 1539 amounted to £262, 19s.

SECTION VI

COLLEGES

1. JESUS.—Was founded by John Poultney, who was several times Lord Mayor of London, in the 20th year of the reign of Edward the Third, near the church of St Lawrence, Poultney, for a master, warden, thirteen priests and four choristers. After the decease of the founder it obtained the name of the College of St Lawrence de Poultney.

2. THE HOLY GHOST or ST MARY was founded on College Hill, by Sir Richard Whittington, mercer and four times Lord Mayor,

in 1418 for a master, four fellows master of arts, clerks, conducts, chorists, etc. Attached to this was an almshouse called 'God's House,' for thirteen poor men. The license for this foundation was granted by King Henry the Fourth, in the eleventh year of his reign, and afterwards confirmed by Henry the Sixth. It was situated in the Vintry and was thereafter called and known by the name of Whittington College. Copies of the original ordinances edicted by the founder are still extant and are interesting in their way. This college escaped by some means the general destruction of all the religious houses during the eighth Henry's reign, though it was suppressed in that of Edward the Sixth.

3. ST MICHAEL'S.—Situated in Crooked Lane, was founded by Sir William Walworth in the year 1380 for a master and nine priests. The license for this foundation was granted by Richard the Second, in the same year. The church attached to it—subsequently the parish one—was a handsome structure, containing many handsome monuments and curious epitaphs.

4. LONDON COLLEGE. — Founded by Peter

Fanlove, Adam Francis and Henry Frowick in the year 1299, adjoining Guildhall, in the old parish of St Foster.

5. ST MARTIN'S-LE-GRAND was first founded in 700, by Wythred, King of Kent, and re-founded in the year 1056, for Augustine Canons by Ingelric and Girard. It was confirmed by William the Conqueror in 1068. It was dedi-cated to St Martin with the addition of *Le Grand,* from the great or extraordinary privi-leges of sanctuary granted through preceding reigns. Among the numerous charters pertain-ing to this house, those especially remarkable were granted in the reigns of William the Conqueror, Henry III, Henry IV, Edward I and Henry VI. It had sax, sol, tol and all the long list of Saxon indulgences. From certain regula-tions laid down by the charter granted in Henry the Sixth's reign it would appear that this sanctuary had previously been the scene of great disorders and a shelter for the lowest class of rogues, ruffians and felons. The question of sanctuary was often raised, but as often settled in favour of the college authorities. Here as well as at the churches of Bow, St Giles and

Barking a curfew bell was nightly tolled. It is described as being a great bell, and was capable of being heard throughout the city. In Edward the First's reign none of the citizens were allowed abroad after that sentinel of the night had sounded. This church and college, this *imperium in imperio*, became one of the numerous possessions of the wealthy Abbey of Westminster. It would appear that a great legal contention respecting the rights and extent of this sanctuary, commenced in the reign of Henry the Sixth, and continued off and on up till the twenty-seventh year of the reign of Henry the Eighth. This house also survived until Edward the Sixth's reign, when in the year 1548 it was surrendered. The liberties of the place, however, still remained, and from time to time very cautiously preserved. A portion of the district still pertains among the possessions of the Dean and Chapter of Westminster.

SECTION VII

HOSPITALS

1. The Savoy. — This hospital was reared upon the ruins of a magnificent palace built by Henry, Earl of Lancaster, about the year 1328, and destroyed by Wat Tyler in 1381. It was founded by Henry VII, and refounded by Henry VIII, in 1511. The latter by his Charter of the 5th July, 1513 constituted the governors a body corporate to consist of a master, five secular chaplains and four regulars in honour of Jesus Christ, of His Mother, and of St John the Baptist. This foundation was denominated 'The Hospital of King Henry VII, late King of England, of the Savoy.' It was suppressed by Edward VI, in 1553, when its revenues amounted to £529, 15s 7d. It was refounded in Queen Mary's reign in 1557, but again and finally suppressed in that of Queen Elizabeth.

2. ST JAMES.—On the site of the present palace of St James stood the hospital of that name. It was founded a considerable time previous to the conquest, by the citizens of London for leprous maids. In subsequent years divers grants of lands and tenements by the benevolent enriched the revenues of this house, and Edward the First granted the privilege of an annual seven days' fair to begin on the eve of St James' festival. Eight brethren had been previously placed on the foundation for the due performance of religious rites. It was surrendered to Henry VIII in the year 1532, when he began to pull it down and eventually erected on the site a portion of the present palace, under its then designation of the manor of St James. Some portions of the ancient hospital it is affirmed can still be traced.

3. ST THOMAS, SOUTHWARK.—This great hospital owes its origin to the fire that destroyed the Priory of St Marie Overie. The Canons erected a temporary structure until their monastery should be rebuilt. When that was done, Peter de Rupibus, Bishop of Winchester, fitted up the temporary building as a hospital and

K

subsequently for the obtaining of better air and
water removed it to the Borough, and having
dedicated the same to St Thomas the apostle,
endowed it with land and tenements of the
annual value of £343. It was surrendered in
1538. Whereupon, among other property, it
was purchased from Henry VIII by the citizens
of London, who repaired and enlarged it at the
cost of £1100. Among the exigencies of the
'Iron Age,' the foundation has been removed to
a pleasanter and more healthy site.

4. St Mary's, Spittal.—Situated in Norton
Folgate, and in the parish of St Botolph, this
priory and hospital was founded by Walter
Brune and Rosia his wife, for canons regular, in
the year 1179. Walter, Archdeacon of London
laid the first stone, and William then Bishop of
London dedicated it to the honour of Jesus
Christ and His Mother, the perpetual Virgin
Mary, by the name of, '*Donus Dei et Beatæ
Mariæ extra Bishopsgate.*' The priory of
Bikenacar in Essex was appropriated and emor-
tified by one of the priors, to the use of this
foundation. The brethren were worthily famed
for their bounty to the poor. This conventual

house was dissolved about the year 1538, at which time there were found 180 well-furnished beds for the relief of the poor. Within an enclosure adjoining the conventual church, stood a carved stone pulpit, termed a cross like unto that which stood for so long without St Paul's. Regular preachers with fixed stipends were at one time appointed to deliver sermons from these crosses of St Paul's, and St Mary's, Spittal.

5. ST THOMAS OF ACON.—This hospital was situated in Cheapside, between the Old Jewry and Ironmonger Lane, and was founded in the year 1170 by Thomas Fitz-Theobald de Heiley and his wife Agnes, sister to Thomas à Becket, to whom the structure was dedicated. Attached to it was the charnel of St Nicholas and the chapel of St Stephen. The image of the saint stood in a niche over the gateway and remained till the reign of Elizabeth, when it was overthrown. It was well endowed by its founder, and subsequently received additional sources of income by gifts and bequests. The master and brethren also acquired a beautiful chapel on the other side of the old Jewry and received permission from Henry the Eighth to erect a

covered gallery across the street to connect
the two establishments, and subsequently on St
Peter's Night, 1536, from this very gallery, the
King and Queen beheld the marching watch set
out. In the conventual chapel, the learned
Italian, Antonio de Dominis, Archbishop of
Spoletto, preached divers sermons in the Italian
language. From this church also used to issue
the procession on Lord Mayor's Day. This
house was surrendered to Henry the Eighth, on
the 21st October, 1538, when its revenues
are stated by Dugdale to have amounted to
£277, 3s 4d. It was subsequently purchased by
Sir Thomas Gresham on behalf of the Mercer's
Company.

6. ST GILES IN THE FIELDS was founded
and endowed for leprous patients by Queen
Matilda, consort to Henry the First and
daughter of Malcolm, King of Scotland, in the
year 1117. Henry the Second confirmed all the
previous benefactions and further endowed it.
Edward the Third, by his charter, granted this
hospital to the master and brethren of the order
of Burton St Lazar of Jerusalem, in Leicestershire, whereupon it became a cell subject to the

said Burton St Lazar. At the foot of the garden belonging to this foundation, stood the public gallows, for a considerable number of years, and on their way to execution the condemned were allowed to rest at this hospital and partake of their last refreshment, in the shape of a large measure of ale out of 'St Giles Bowl.' It was dissolved in the year 1543 and soon after granted by Henry the Eighth to Lord Dudley. The conventual chapel was saved and a portion of it stands to the present day embodied in the parish church.

7. St Bartholomew's.—This foundation, as before stated, was by Rahere, the minstrel of Henry the First. It was governed by a master, eight brethren and four sisters. It became by successive grants richly endowed, and upon its suppression in 1539, its revenues reached nearly £1000, a sum equal to quite £5000 in the present day. In the last year of his reign Henry the Eighth refounded the hospital which at present exists as one of our largest institutions, while the building embodies some of the finest portions of the ancient Priory and Hospital.

8. The Temple.—This house was founded by the

Knights Templars originally in Oldbourn—then called the 'Old Temple'—in the reign of King Stephen, and subsequently on its present site in Fleet Street, in the year 1185, during the reign of Henry II, when it was called the 'New Temple.' The beautiful church, standing in all its matchless beauty to the present day, was built upon the model of that of the Holy Sepulchre and was dedicated to God and our Blessed Lady. It was consecrated in 1185 by Heraclius, Patriarch of the church called the Holy Resurrection at Jerusalem. This house was often made the storehouse for treasure belonging to divers persons. In 1240 this temple was re-edified and rededicated. In 1245 Pope Innocent's Nuncio took up his residence within the conventual premises. These Knights Templars, from being originally poor, became, by divers numerous grants and benefactions, the wealthiest and haughtiest community in the kingdom. They possessed temples at Cambridge, Bristol, Canterbury, Dover, Warwick and at divers other places. They entertained, at different times, in a most sumptuous manner, the nobility, ambassadors, and other notable personages. Many remarkable Parliaments and important Councils were held within this august house. In the year 1308, all the Templars in England and in other parts of Christendom were, for divers important State reasons, apprehended and committed to prison, and in the year 1310 were tried before a Council holden in their Temple in Fleet Street, upon several counts, the most important and irrefutable of which was that of heresy, and upon which they were condemned to perpetual penance amid certain selected monasteries, where, we are informed, they behaved themselves modestly. By a Council held at Vienna in 1324 all the possessions of the Knights Templars were given to the Knights Hospitallers of the order of St John the Baptist, called St John of Jerusalem. This gift was, to the extent of the English possessions, ratified by Edward the Third. But in the same reign these Knights Hospitallers granted the Temple in Fleet Street to the students of the Common Laws, in whose hands it has remained ever since. It would appear that the Knights Templars at first wore a simple garb of white, but in Pope Eugenius' time they assumed a large crimson cross over the white robe.

SECTION VIII

FRATERNITIES OR GUILDS

1. ALLHALLOWS, BARKING.—A fraternity was founded here by John, Earl of Worcester, cousin to Edward the Fourth. To this foundation was attached a beautiful chapel, erected by Richard the First, and beneath the high altar of which his heart was subsequently deposited. The same Earl of Worcester gave to the '*custos*' of this fraternity the Priory of Totingbroke, the advowson of the parish church of Stretham, in the county of Surrey, and a part of the Priory of Okebarne, in Wiltshire. He directed this foundation to be called the King's Chapel or Chantry, '*In Capella beatæ Mariæ de Barking.*' King Richard the Third rebuilt this Conventual Cell, and refounded it for a College of Priests,

consisting of a dean and six canons. The first Dean was Edward Chatterton, one of the King's especial favourites. This foundation was suppressed and pulled down in 1548.

2. LEADENHALL.—Attached to the original market, erected in 1444, by one Simon Eyre, a citizen of London, was a large and handsome chapel, wherein was founded, in 1460, a fraternity of the Trinity of sixty priests, by William Rome, John Risby and Thomas Ashby, priests, under a special license from Edward the Fourth. In the year 1512, the mayor and commonalty confirmed the rights of this foundation. It was a common usage for those priests to celebrate divine service in their chapel every market day.

3. ST PETERS.—It appears a fraternity was founded in Cornhill, close to the ancient corn market, by William Kingston, about the year 1298, for the education of the youth of the city. A portion of the church attached to this foundation appears to have belonged to a very ancient ecclesiastical structure, asserted by some authorities* still extant, to have been the first Christian Temple in Great Britain.

* Bede's Ecc. Hist.

4. St Augustine's, Papey.—This religious house was situated close to the city walls, near the north end of St Mary's Axe, and was founded in 1430, by William Oliver, William Barnebie and John Stafford, for a master, two wardens, chaplains, chauntry priests, conducts, and other brethren and sisters. The brethren of this house suffered great poverty, and were relieved by the alms of the charitable. They had a peculiar duty attached to their vocation, in attending at all great funerals, and in singing dirges, for which they received substantial bequests. The church attached to this foundation, called St Augustine-in-the-wall, was, with tenements and land adjoining, assigned to these poor priests of the Papey by the deed poll of one Richard Wodehouse, Prior of the neighbouring monastery of the Holy Trinity. It was dedicated to the Holy and Undivided Trinity, the Father, Son and Holy Ghost, the glorious Virgin Mary, St Charity and St John the Evangelist. This brotherhood was suppressed in King Edward the Sixth's reign, and the church and conventual buildings pulled down.

5. The Holy Trinity.—Originally a monastic

hospital, it was suppressed with other alien houses by Henry V, and its revenues were granted to the parish of St Botolph, on condition that in the church was founded a fraternity dedicated to the Holy Trinity. It was situated at the corner of Little Britain, in Aldersgate Street and some portions of the ancient buildings were standing so late as the commencement of the present century. It was subject to the rules and sway of the Prior and Canons of St Mary Overie, with which Monastery it was simultaneously dissolved.

6. St Catharine's.—Situated to the east of the Tower, in the district known as Wapping, this house was founded by Matilda, the Queen of King Stephen, by license of the Prior and Convent of the Holy Trinity, on whose land it was erected. Queen Elinor, wife of Edward I, became a second foundress, and appointed a master, three brethren, and three sisters, ten poor women and six poor men. She endowed it with the Manors of Carleton, in Wiltshire, and Upchurch in Kent. A third foundress afterwards appeared in Queen Philippa, wife to Edward III, who in 1351, created it a Chauntry.

It was subsequently styled a free chapel, a college, and a hospital for poor sisters. It rose in favour and became richly endowed, receiving in addition to the gifts above recorded, the Manors of Rishendon, in the Isle of Shepy, of Chesingbery, in Wilts, and Quarley, in Southampton, parcel of the Priory of Okeburn, and tenements near Reynham, in Kent. Many liberties were during divers reigns granted to this foundation. King Henry VIII and Queen Catharine, were liberal patrons. Many very high and honourable persons became members of the fraternity, among whom was the great Cardinal. Within the precincts was a district called the Jewry, which was sacred as a Sanctuary for apostate Jews. Also within its walls were several breweries and manufactories. It was surrendered in Edward the Sixth's reign, when its revenues amounted to £315, 14s 2d.

7. St James', Garlickhithe.—This fraternity of poor brethren and sisters was founded in the year 1375 to 'the honour of God our Creator, His Mother St Mary, All Hallows, and St James the Apostle.' The privileges of the Guild were open to anyone desirous of living as a recluse

upon paying an entrance fee of 6s 8d, and sub-
scribing a yearly donation of 2s and an additional 1s 8d on the eve of their yearly feast,
being the Sunday after the day of St James the
Apostle. The foundation was otherwise sup-
ported by the contributions of the charitable.
It was suppressed in the reign of Edward the
Sixth.

8. ST JAMES-IN-THE-WALL.—So called from its
being situate in London Wall, at the north-west
corner of Monkwell Street. The fraternity was
founded during the reign of Edward the First
for indigent monks. It belonged to the Abbot
and convent of Gerandon or Garendon in
Leicestershire. In the chapel the company of
clothworkers attended to hear special discourses
on four festival days in the year, viz., the
Annunciation, St John the Baptist, St Michael
and St Thomas; upon which occasions they
would disburse their charity among the poor
brethren. It was dissolved in 1538 by Henry
the Eighth, by whom it was subsequently
granted to William Lamb, the citizen who
erected the famed conduit near the present
Foundling Hospital.

9. St Mary, Rouncival.—On the site where lately stood Northumberland House, and within the rustic village of Charing stood this hermitage. It was founded by William Marshall, Earl of Pembroke, during the reign of Henry the Third. It was a cell to a Priory of the name in Navarre in France ; but being suppressed among the alien priories by Henry the Fifth, it was refounded by Edward the Fourth in 1476. It was again and finally suppressed by Edward the Sixth, who granted it to Sir Thomas Cawarden, to be held in soccage of the Abbey of Westminster. Subsequently it came into the hands of Henry Howard, Earl of Northampton, who erected on the site the late stately edifice of Northumberland House.

10. St Catharine's Crutched Friars.— Here, in the year 1415, was founded a Guild of Dutch brethren and sisters. The rules and ordinances pertaining to its government were the subject of a special decree by Richard Blodywell, D.S., the Commissary of London, on 25th October 1495. There was an entrance fee and an annual subscription. New rulers were appointed on its festival day of St Catharine in

each year, at which time also new members were admitted.

11. THE HOLY BLOOD OF WILSNACK.—This fraternity was also situate in Crutched Friars, and was of Dutch foundation. It was originated during the reign of Henry the Sixth, with the avowed object of engendering love and peace among good Christian people, and was dedicated to the special honour of the Holy Blood of Wilsnack and of all the saints in heaven. The annual day of festival and assize among this brotherhood was held on Holy Rode day, the 3rd May. The rule of conduct and mode of life were very strict. These two last foundations survived the general dissolution of religious houses some years, unto 1559.

12. ALL SOULS, ST PAUL'S.—On the north side of St Paul's churchyard stood a large charnel house, and over it a chapel of very ancient foundation. This erection having got into a bad state of repair was given over by the Archbishop of Canterbury, in the year 1379, to the custody of a fraternity, styling themselves 'All Souls,' upon condition of their restoring the chapel. The duty of this fraternity, was on

certain days of observance, to sing and pray for
the souls and well-being of all Christians, and
once in the year, on the eve of their festival day
of All Souls, to proceed in public procession
through the principal thoroughfares of the city,
in their robes and with lighted torches, ' number-
ing their prayers as they went along, and their
secret orisons, pouring them out *vultu cordiali*,
with a serious countenance for the living and
the dead.'   The chapel was pulled down in the
year 1549, and the bones of the dead carted
away from the charnel-house, when the refuse of
mortality amounted to no less than a thousand
cart loads.

13. KNIGHTEN GUILD. — This establishment
adjoined the Priory of the Holy Trinity and
was of somewhat uncommon origin.   It would
appear from an ancient chronicle that in the
reign of King Edgar, thirteen knights, well-
beloved of king and realm, requested in return
for services they had rendered, a grant of a
piece of land lying waste to the east of the city,
and the liberty to found thereon a guild.   The
king, we are told, granted the request upon
certain conditions, to-wit, 'that each of them

should victoriously accomplish three combats, one above ground, one under ground and the third in water. After this, on a certain day, in East Smithfield, they should run with spears against all comers. All which was gloriously performed.' And the same day the king granted them the land they prayed for and named the fraternity 'The Knighten Guild.' The achievements of such Quixotic conditions should have eternally emblazoned the names of such doughty champions. The guild received a confirmation of its grant and privileges in the reign of Edward the Confessor, and by special charter also of William Rufus. This guild, during the year 1115, merged into the Priory of the Holy Trinity. This amalgamation received the approval of Henry the First by special deed. All these documents were registered in the book of remembrances kept at the Guildhall and can still be traced there.*

14. THE ROLLS.—So called from its being the repository of the Records of the Court of Chancery. It was anciently a *Domus Conversorum*, an establishment for the reception and

* Book 'Dunthorn' in Guildhall Lib., fol. 78.

L.

support of converted Jews, and was with that object founded by Henry the Third about 1233, who built a fair chapel adjoining the Hermitage for their special use. This foundation was numerously patronised and received the countenance and support of Edward the Second. It was governed by certain appointed monks of the Carthusian order. They were very poor and styled themselves *Cœlicolœ Christi*, or Christ's Heavenly Inhabitants. This establishment was dissolved in the year 1377.

THE END

Index

INDEX

—— :o:——

	PAGE		PAGE
ABBEYS,	108	Brevia, The	84
Abbot,	78	Briggitines	18
Actuarius, The	87	Brothers, Rank of	50
Allhallows, Barking	152	Bursar, The	85
All Souls, St Paul's	159		
Almoner, The	83	CANCELLARIUS, THE	87
Almonry	75	Capuchins	18, 50
Altar, splendour of	28	Carmadules, the Sect of	50
Apologues, Two	37	Carmelites	18, 50
Archives	81	Carthusians	18
Architects, Monastic	28	Celestines, the Sect of	50
Augustines, The	18, 133	Cellarer, The	80
Austerity	48	Cells	77
Austin Friars	133	Chamberlain, The	84
		Chapter House	69
BAKEHOUSE, THE	76	Charity of the Monks	91
Barnabites	51	Charterhouse Abbey	115
Belief in Miracles	60	Choir, the glories of	28
Benedictines, The	18	Church, The	68
Benefits bestowed	45	Cistercians	18, 50
Black Book, The	95	Claustral, The	80
Black Friars, The	20, 49	Clerkenwell Nunnery	139
Blackfriars' Monastery	128	Classification of Orders	50
Boys	89	Cloister	48, 71

	PAGE
Cluny, the Sect of	50
Code of Monachism	51
Colleges	140
Commentary on the Monks	45
Completorium (complins)	56
Convents	108
Configuration of Church Interiors	25
Conventuals	18
Corporals, The	83
Crusades, The	47
Crutched Friars' Monastery	132
DAILY DUTIES	53
Demerits of the Monks	61, 89
Description of Churches	27
Diet and Dress of Monks	51
Digest of Monastic Houses	107
Discipline, Monastic	40
Disruption of Monasteries	101
Dominican Privileges	24
Dominican Saints	21
Dominicans, The	19
Dormitory	56, 71
Dress of the Monks	23
Druids	47
EASTMINSTER ABBEY	116
Elsing Priory	117
Endowments	25
Epitome of London Monasteries	108

	PAGE
Erudition, Monastic	98
Eudistes, the Sect of the	51
Exchequer	76
Explorator, The	87
Extravagances	65
FESTIVALS	64
Fontevrault, the Sect of	50
Franciscans	18
Franciscan Privileges	24
Fraternities	152
Friaries	128
GLORIES OF THE PAST, MONASTIC	33
Granaterius, The	87
Grandmont, the Sect of	50
Granges, The	77
Great Monkish Painters	28
Grey Friars, The	20, 49
Grey Friars' Monastery	131
Guest Hall	73
Guilds	152
HAVENS OF REFUGE	49
High Mass, the Office of	55
Holy Blood of Wilsnack	159
Holy Ghost College	140
Holy Trinity Guild	154
Holy Trinity Priory	118
Host, the Office of the	83
Hospitaller, The	85

	PAGE		PAGE
Hospitals	144	Lying House . .	77
Hostrey, The . . .	73		
Humility of the Monks .	90	MANNERS AND CUSTOMS	51
		Martyrology, The . .	81
IMPERFECTIONS, MONKISH	92	Master of the Novices .	86
Infirmarer, The . .	85	Matins, the Office of .	55
Infirmary	74	Mausoleums . . .	100
In Memoriam . . .	34	Mendicant Orders . .	19, 91
Inns, Monastic . . .	58	Merits of the Monks .	89
Interior of churches most		Minimes . . .	18
dazzling . . .	28	Minories Nunnery . .	138
Introduction of Monachism		Misericord, the Office of	76
into England . . .	47	Mint	76
		Monachism, Errors of .	92
JANITOR, THE . . .	86	Monastic Buildings .	25
Jeronymites, The . .	19	Monastic Courts of Justice	69
Jesuits	19	Monitores . . .	79
Jesus College . . .	140	Monks, Orders of . .	50
		Mortifications . .	51
KITCHEN	76	Museum . . .	73
Kitchener, The . .	82		
Knighten Guild . .	160	NONES, THE OFFICE OF .	56
		Novices	89
LARDENARIUS, THE . .	88	Novitiate . . .	89
Lauds, the Office of . .	55	Nunneries . . .	136
Lazarists, the Sect of .	51		
Leadenhall Guild . .	153	OATH, THE MONASTIC .	63
Lecturer, The . . .	86	Obedientiaries, The .	87
Lectures at Meals . .	36	Observants . . .	18
Legends . . .	37, 38	Officers of Monasteries .	78
Library	73	Offices in Monasteries .	68
Locutory . . .	74, 84	Operarius, The . .	87
London College . . .	141	Oratorians, The Sect of	51

	PAGE
Orcharder, The	87
Orders of Monks	18
Ostentation, Monastic	97
PAINTERS, MONKISH	18, 28
Palaces of Art, Monastic	28
Part I	15
Part II	43
Part III	105
Patrons of Art	59
Pittancer, The	84
Polytheism	62
Pontificals	64
Porcarius, The	87
Preaching Friars	66
Precentor, The	81
Preface	7
Premontré, The Sect of	50
Prior, The	79
Prime, The Office of	55
Priories	117
Prophecy	60
Protector Somerset, The	113
RECOLLETS, THE SECT OF THE	50
Refectioner, The	84
Refectory	56, 70
Registrarius, The	87
Regular Canons	50
Regular Clerks	51
Relics	29
Research, Monastic	64

	PAGE
Rise and Progress of Monachism	47
Ritualism	33
Rolls Guild, The	161
Rood, Changes in The	32
Rood, Legends of the	30
Rosary, The	21
Ruling Principles	51
SACRIST, THE	82
St Alberte of Vercelli (Carmelites)	19
St Augustine (Augustines)	18
St Augustine's Papey Guild	154
St Bartholomew Hospital	149
St Bartholomew Priory	120
St Basil	50
St Benedict (Benedictines)	18, 50
St Bridget of Sweden	18
St Catharine's, Crutched Friars	158
St Catharine's Guild	155
St Dominick (Dominicans)	19, 21
St Francis (Franciscans)	18
St Giles-in-the-fields Hospital	148
St Helen's Nunnery	137
St Ignatius Loyola (Jesuits)	19

	PAGE		PAGE
St James Garlickhithe .	156	Silence . .	54
St James Hospital	145	Song School . .	77
St James-in-the-Wall .	157	Sorcerers . . .	62
St Jerome (Jeronymites)	19	Splendour, Conventual . 33, 58	
St John the Baptist		Subchantor, The .	81
Nunnery . . .	136	Subprior, The	80
St John's Priory . .	125	Subsacrist, The . .	83
St Joseph (Augustines)	18	Subseneschal, The .	83
St Martin's-le-grand College		Sulpiciens, The Sect of the	51
lege	142	Sumptuousness of	
St Mary Bethelem Priory	124	Churches, The . .	25
St Mary Overie Priory .	122	Survey, General Monastic	17
St Mary Rouncival .	158	Superstition . .	60
St Mary Spittal Hospital	146		
St Michael's College .	141	TASTE IN MONKS , .	57
St Peter's Guild . .	153	Temple Hospital, The .	149
St Peter Nolasco (Order		Terrier of the House, The	88
of Mercy) . . .	18	Tierce, The office of .	55
St Philip Benozzi (Servi)	18	Theatins, The Sect of .	51
St Saviour's Abbey .	114		
St Thomas of Acon Hospital		VANDALISM . . .	103
pital	147	Vespers, The Office of .	56
St Thomas Southwark		Vestiary . . .	78
Hospital . . .	145	Vigilarius, The . .	87
Sanctuary . . 49, 77, 136		Virgultarius . .	87
Savoy Hospital . .	144	Visitors, Rules for	73
Scriptorium . . .	71		
Sempectæ, The . .	88	WEALTH OF THE MONKS	25
Seneschal, The . .	83	Westminster Abbey .	108
Seniors, The . . .	88	Westminster City .	112
Servi, The . . .	18	White Friars Monastery	134
Sext, The Office of	56	White Friars, Order of .	134
Services, Continuous .	100		

www.ingramcontent.com/pod-product-compliance
Lightning Source LLC
Chambersburg PA
CBHW020012030726
47500CB00002B/544